Contemporary Issues of Indian Economy

Contemporary Issues of Indian Economy

Dhirendra Nath Konar

AKANSHA PUBLISHING HOUSE
NEW DELHI-110002 (INDIA)

AKANSHA PUBLISHING HOUSE
4649-B/21, Ansari Road
Darya Ganj, New Delhi - 110 002
Ph.: 23263193 / 9811582579 / 09435116718
Telefax: 011-23263193
Email: ektabooks@yahoo.com

Contemporary Issues of Indian Economy

First Published 2009
ISBN 978-81-8370-167-9

PRINTED IN INDIA

Published by Akansha Publishing House, New Delhi and Printed at Aryan Enterprises, Delhi.

Dedicated
To
the Memory of My
Father NIRANJAN and Mother
SHUBHADRA

Contents

Preface

The present volume under the caption "Contemporary Issues of Indian Economy" is a collection of research articles presented by me in different seminars and conferences both inside and outside India. Almost each and every article covered in this volume has been published in different journals in either abstract or full form. The contents of many articles presented in this volume have been changed. I have tried to make the information as current as possible. However, due to shortage of time in some cases this has not been possible and for this the author may be graciously excused.

Poverty, especially, the rural one, has pained me very much since my birth in rural Bengal. I have seen in my own eyes how many members of different families had to pass their days almost being half-fed. This is, especially, true to the elderly women of the families I am speaking about. These women after distributing almost the entire food prepared by themselves among the children and other members of the family, had to be satisfied only with the little left-over. But such women had, smilingly, borne with it for days together. They did not make any protest for it because they were fully aware of their financial condition. Children and other members of the family, in most cases, failed to get iota of trace of it, though this was a grim reality.

Today there has been some change in the matter just described. But still there is the problem of poverty, malnutrition, unemployment, illiteracy and inequality. Some such aspects have, very mildly, been brought out in the present volume. Poverty can not be eliminated through charity—it can be eliminated only if the people themselves can earn their bread by the sweat of their brow. Some such prescriptions have been advocated in different sections of this book. If the general readers go through the present volume and understand the problem of the people of the society, my effort in jotting down these information will be considered to be amply rewarded.

In preparing this volume my two engineer sons and their mother have given me constant pressure and encouragement.

I am sincerely thankful to Mr. M.P. Misra, Akansha Publishing House, New Delhi, who had taken the responsibility of bringing out the present volume within a very short period of time.

Dhirendra Nath Konar

1

Introduction

The immortal poet Kalidas before writing his renowned book "Raghuvansha" (in Sanskrit) bowed to God Shiva and Goddess Parvati and said, "Let me invoke the Father (Parameshwara) and Mother (Parvati) of the whole world. By taking their blessings, he had, successfully, completed his famous work. Kautilya, the great administrator, economist, political thinker and the statesman of ancient India, has become immortal by writing his invaluable book "*Arthashastra*" which contains almost every aspect of modern Economics. But people with their very short-spanned memory forgot such a great name. After the rediscovery of *Arthashastra* people have, again, been talking much of such a great personality. Unhesitatingly, one of the contemporary issues of Indian economy is Kautilya who, according to our opinion, heads the list of such issues of the Indian Economy. This has been put in Chapter two, Chapter one being the introduction.

A second contemporary issue that India has been facing is corruption which is so rampant in the far and near of the whole economy. It has, rightly, been said by Lord Linton: "Power corrupts and absolute power corrupts absolutely." This is very much vivid in both the States and Union

Territories. Our third chapter has been devoted to a brief description of corruption and economic growth in the context of a developing economy.

There can be no denying the fact that women can play a significant role in the construction of the National Economy. Women, actually, play a very vital role in bringing peace, harmony and tranquillity in our family life. Pandit Jawaharlal Nehru, our first Prime Minister, once said that women are the harbinger of modern economic growth. However, very often, we turn a deaf ear to it and fail to treat with them in the way it is expected. This is unethical and undesirable, too. One glaring example of our apathetic attitude towards women in our country is the continuous decline in the female-male ratio, generally called the sex ratio (the number of females per one thousand of males) between 1901 and 2001. Another very terrible feature of our utter negligence of women in our country is the gradual decline in the child sex ratio. Unless this is checked there will be disruption in the social harmony. We should bear this in mind and do the needful at the earliest. In this context it is worth mentioning that women can, greatly, help us in controlling the present high growth rate of population, which has been eating into the fruits of development reaped by our country. It is a fact that we are badly in need of arresting the present trend growth rate of population of India. Keeping this idea in mind we have incorporated the topic captioned "Women's role in the present high growth of population in India" in the list of contemporary issues of the Indian Economy.

Chapter five captioned "Trend of Indian Agriculture in the Post-Independence Period" also falls in the category of contemporary issues of Indian Economy. It is true that Indian Economy, even in the twenty first century, falls back upon agriculture. Though the contribution of agriculture to the Gross Domestic Product (GDP) in our country has, gradually, been declining, its sector-wise importance in our economy is the supreme so far as the employment of work-force is concerned. During the reform period our agriculture has not flourished to the extent it was expected. As a consequence, many untoward incidents have taken root in the entire economy. Hence various aspects of agriculture in India have been presented in this chapter.

Indian Economy is still now rural in nature. But the rural people, at least those living in the base of the pyramid consisting of the scenario of the rural economy, do not get a square meal a day and this has been happening even in the twenty first century full of computer, fax, e-mail, internet, cell phone and what not. Thus reduction in rural poverty is a must. Hence another contemporary issue of Indian Economy is rural poverty and its removal. So the sixth chapter has been captioned "The extent of Poverty in India".

It may be said that a new era in Indian Economy has started with the introduction of economic reforms in our country since 1991. Naturally, a very very contemporary issue of our economy is economic reforms and its success, especially with regard to the generation of employment which is a very burning issue. Therefore, the seventh chapter headed by "Economic Reforms, Employment Generation and Regional Disparity in India" has been devoted to examine to what extent the economic reforms have been congenial to the creation of employment opportunities and whether regional disparity during this period has lessened or gone increasing.

Of late, the role of the service sector has, steeply, been increasing. This is quite in tune with the nature of development being experienced by both the developed and developing countries. India has not been an exception to this very common experience. Colin Clark, the famous development economist, had, long ago, foreseen that with the progress of time the importance of the primary sector will come down, that of the secondary sector will, gradually, increase and that of the tertiary sector will, quickly, expand. This is the experience gathered by some countries of Asia, like China, Indonesia, Taiwan, Malaysia, South Korea, Pakistan and India. However, this is the experience with regard to the contribution of various sectors to the GDP of the countries concerned. But together with the attainment of this common experience there is, however, a new experience: the importance of the primary sector to the GDP has, steeply, fallen though the percentage of work-force to this sector has come down very insignificantly. As a result, the rural people are being seriously hurt. We have tried to show this in the eighth chapter entitled "Impact of the Service-led Growth on Indian Economy" which is, obviously, a highly relevant contemporary issue of our economy.

It is, undoubtedly, true that global warming is a very contemporary issue in not only India but also all over the world. In fact, global warming is a much talked-about issue across the world and people all through the world has been thinking about how to get rid of it. Keeping this global feeling in mind, we have put the ninth chapter under the title "Population Growth, Global Warming and Economic Development". Our contention is that the very high growth of population all over the world, especially, in the developing countries, is one of the fundamental reasons behind this warming. Both the developed and the developing countries have been putting continuous pressure on our "Mother Earth". Our sense to this direction dawned as early as 1972 since when about 36 years have passed. But we have not taken enough steps to pacify our "Universal Mother" and we have been facing the consequences. Unless proper steps are taken, the whole civilization will have to bear unbearable troubles.

Another contemporary issue is the World Trade Organization formed in 1995 since when thirteen years have passed. So the tenth chapter headed by "WTO and its Impact on Indian Foreign Trade with Special Reference to the Agricultural Sector" has been placed in the present volume as one of the contemporary issues of the Indian Economy. Here we have studied the impact of the WTO on the agriculture-based international trade. The reason is that since India is rich in agriculture, it is expected that we may nourish in the external front in the sphere of agriculture also. That will be viewed in this chapter. Naturally, there will be some recommendations for the furtherance of this trade.

The eleventh chapter under the caption "Regional Co-operation for a Better Indian Economy" is very much a contemporary issue of our economy. To get more growth, more employment and even more income, co-operation among various countries of the world has always been an avowed principle. By adhering to this principle a very important regional co-operation had been formed in 1985 by seven South Asian countries. More than twenty three years have passed since the formation of the SAARC. Hence time has become ripe to review the balance sheet of participating in the regional co-operation. This will be clear if this chapter is gone through with a bit attention.

The book ends, finally, with the twelfth chapter entitled "The Extent of Human Poverty in India and Indonesia." The general readers may, suddenly, get surprised at the title of this chapter and its inclusion in the present volume. However, such surprise will be dispelled as soon as they, very keenly, go through this chapter. Any study between India and Indonesia may itself be highly interesting in that there are some similarities between these two countries. Both the countries having been under foreign rule for centuries had become sovereign States almost at the same time (India in August 1947 and Indonesia in December 1949). Both the countries are very populous—India is the second most populous country while Indonesia is the fourth such country. In spite of some similarities between the two countries the nature of development attained by these two countries is quite different. Indonesia after overcoming the initial hurdles has emerged to be a very prosperous nation. Today Indonesia is sometimes called "a cub of Asia", though India is yet to acquire such a name. This means that India is to learn something from Indonesia.

The book ends with a concluding chapter called "Conclusion" which just highlights the conclusions that may be drawn from the previous chapters just mentioned.

2

Kautilya: The Great Indian Economic Thinker in Ancient Times

[Abstract

Kautilya also known as Chanakya and Vishnugupta and a contemporary of Aristotle has been familiar with the whole world for his treatise "Arthashastra" (written in Cir.300 B.C.). A practical politician, a shrewd statesman and a unique secular law giver of ancient India, he was a great political scientist. In spite of his belief in monarchy, he was socialistic in his approach and ideas. Though he was a ruthless administrator he was humane and sympathetic to the downtrodden.

Arthashastra is a masterpiece work in the context of economic ideas. Kautilya's ultimate objective was to create a Welfare State that will benefit not the king but the people. He was an ardent advocate of the introduction of social security measures for some people. His treatise is the first ever spelt out document about the principles and practices of Public Finance. His canons of taxation are still modern. He was strongly in favour of introducing economic planning basically for the creation of wealth of the State. His treatment on differential rates of interest brings out his acute sense of grim reality.

From various considerations we may, unambiguously, state that some of the traits of modern economic thinking can be traced in Kautilya. In the History of Economic Thought we owe much to Aristotle for being the earliest economic thinker. We wish Kautilya should also be paid similar tribute. It is our conviction that many economic ideas developed after Kautilya have been, greatly, influenced by the economic ideas proclaimed by Kautilya and in this sense he can, really, be said to be a forerunner of modern economic ideas. We also conclude that Kautilya is great but rediscovered Kautilya is still greater.]

Introduction

a) *Kautilya: The Man*

Kautilya also known as Chanakya and Vishnugupta and a contemporary of Aristotle, the ancient Greek economic thinker, has been known to the whole world for his immortal work entitled "Arthashastra". A practical politician, a shrewd statesman and a unique secular law giver of ancient India he was a great political scientist. In spite of his belief in monarchy, he was socialistic in his approach and ideas. Though he was a ruthless administrator, he was humane and sympathetic to the downtrodden. He became a counselor and advisor to King Chandragupta (reigning c.321 - c.297 BC) of the Mauryan Empire of Southern India but simply lived himself. His *Arthashastra*, containing fifteen sections, each one of them dealing with a phase of Government, came to be Chandragupta's guide. He has been very often condemned for wisdom and knowledge of human nature. All authorities agree, however, that it was mainly because of Kautilya that the Maurya Empire under Chandragupta and later Asoka (reigning c 265 - c 238 BC) had become a model of efficient Government.

b) *Arthashastra: Lost and Rediscovered*

Kautilya's economic ideas have well been presented in his *Arthashastra* that was written in Cir 300 B.C. But, the content of the glorious book was not known to the Indians, let alone the world before 1902 the year when a pandit from Tanjore handed over the manuscript to Dr. Shama Sastry, the then Librarian of the Oriental Manuscripts Library, Mysore. No sooner had Dr. Sastry published the full text of *Arthashastra* in 1909 than it generated much enthusiasm and interest among various scholars in both India and abroad. Then and there a vast body of literature on Kautilya's *Arthashastra* started flourishing. The English version of this book in 1914 made it known to the western world. However, in India especially after Independence the interest in the study of this profound source of knowledge of Economics subsided and the text was relegated mainly to the students of Sanskrit Literature. Surprisingly enough, outside India, it is held in high esteem and it is a part of the syllabi of the Military Academics and Espionage Agencies of many a country of the world.

Most people of India may have an idea that perhaps Kautilya's *Arthashastra* is the only significant Indian discourse on Economics and Public Administration. But this is far from reality as Kautilya had himself asserted that his treatise *Arthashastra* was a compendium of almost all *Arthashastras* composed by earlier scholars as well as his own contributions. This itself is a testimony to the fact that in India Economics was developed long before Kautilya. However, Kautilya was known and followed by many scholars. This may be pointed out by the fact that *Nitishastra* by Kamandaka duly acknowledged *Arthashastra* as his reference in 800 A.D. However, like many sources of ancient Indian knowledge, *Arthashastra* was rediscovered in 1902 and became known to the world.

Economic Ideas Contained in Arthashastra

Arthashastra by Kautilya is a masterpiece work especially in the context of time when the book was written. Kautilya had encyclopaedic knowledge about various aspects of governing a monarchy. His acute sense of knowledge about reality has been embodied in his treatise *Arthashastra*, which translated literally means principles of money or wealth. The author, however, used the word in much broader context to incorporate many of the activities of a State, namely social, political, economic, military and others, which may highly influence its wealth. His ultimate objective was to create a Welfare State which will benefit not the king but the people. Naturally, he thought that a strong and wealthy monarchy would be in a position to protect the interest of the people against external aggression by other kings. The establishment of a wealthy State being the principal aim of Kautilya, he had, obviously, framed his economic ideas in such a manner that he could attain that aim. Such ideas revealed through his treatise are, in reality, numerous. In the following paragraphs we shall, very briefly, touch upon some such ideas as are related primarily to money.

Kautilaya's Acumen in Various Fields of Economics

a) *Kautilya on Finance*

According to Kautilya, finances are the foundation of the State which aims at enhancing well being of the people. For generating welfare of the citizens of the State he had laid down the following areas: (i) maintenance and development of "forest, plants, trees, water resources, mines and similar other natural resources, (ii) protection of agriculture, (iii) protection of young boys, women, elderly and the poverty-stricken, (iv) protection against calamities and (v) vigilance over the officials of the State".

For the successful implementation of these schemes finances are badly needed. If, according to the great statesman, finances become weak, revolutions may be incited and the army itself may revolt against the authority. Since all the State functions are dependent on finances, financial distress will seriously jeopardize the State.

b) ***Kautilya on Public Finance***

According to many experts on Public Finance, *Arthashastra* is the first ever seriously spelt out treaties about principles and practices of Public Finance in the framework of a decentralized administrative setup. One of the basic sources of finance is taxation in the field of which he has many underlying principles or canons. The following three canons are explicit in *Arthashastra*.

The first such canon or principle is that the State should recognize the limits to its power of taxation. The State should, clearly, make the distinction between short-term expediency and long-term possibilities of different tax policies. In the short-run, tax rates may be raised to a good extent to meet the situations of emergency. This is, specially, needed when the treasury is not able to meet the sudden demands made on it by war or other contingencies. However, in the long run, the State should not tax the economy indiscreetly. According to him, a heavy dose of taxation would be self-defeating. This is, particularly, true in the frontiers from where the taxpayers could flee to the neighboring countries.

The second canon of taxation is its burdensomeness. The State should, undoubtedly, meet some of its requirements through taxation. But before the imposition of tax, the State must try to keep the cost of collection of tax to the least. This is what the Adam Smithian concept of canon of economy found in his famous treatise *Wealth of Nations* (1776). At the same time the State should help to augment the paying capacity of the economy through judicious manner on social overhead. Moreover, through an appropriate assistance and tax exemptions the State should encourage profitable productive activities.

The third canon of taxation, in the opinion of Kautilya, is that tax increases should be graduated. To increase revenue from taxation, therefore, it is preferable to increase the income base rather than to rely on raising the tax rate.

Besides mentioning the possibilities of raising revenue through imposition of taxation, Kautilya suggested that the overall policy objective of the State was to have a surplus budget. For the attainment of this budget he advocated that there should be an economy in public expenditure and at the same time there should be an increase in revenue.

c) ***Kautilya on Pricing***

An important aspect of Kautilya's economic ideas is with regard to the discussion of pricing. In this sphere the author is able to bring in his analysis of economic behavior in response to various stimuli. His analysis of the determination of price of a commodity and the consequent variation in it has the elements of both demand and supply. He had even written about the estimation of demand and control of supply. In his opinion, a king should, under no circumstances, arbitrarily, fix the price of a product without paying due attention to the demand and supply situations of the product. Obviously, the provision of and an improvement of the means of transport facilitated the flow of goods and affected the pattern of price of the product.

Kautilya was an advocate of the concept of a "just price". This price was designed to maintain the incentive on the part of the business people by allowing them five to ten percent profit in their operations. Since the State-owned businesses competed with the private businesses, some conflict of interest would emerge. To get rid of such a conflict the author advocated that some parity in price should be maintained in such a manner that the private sector did not get any obstruction. He had clearly indicated that while fixing up the price of a product, due attention should be paid to the cost of production, the ratio of supply to demand and also a reasonable level of profit.

In case there was a glut of any commodity, the State was expected to intervene and centralize the sale of that commodity so that the price did not come to the floor.

Apparently, the entire supply was purchased and its sale carried out through the agency of the State at a fixed price.

d) ***Kautilya on Planning***

We have already stated that the basic objective of the State, in the opinion of Kautilya, is to increase the welfare of the people. Keeping this idea in mind, he thought of introducing economic planning for the creation of wealth of the State so that its strength might be improved and at the same time people get due protection and their lot be benefited.

While framing the scheme of economic planning he tried to cover the following major functions of his statecraft:

1) Conservation of resources of urban and rural people,
2) Allocation and utilization of resources for economic growth,
3) Defence of the State, and
4) Consolidation of its potential for emergencies and against attack from external forces.

To make such a scheme of planning successful, the responsibilities had been entrusted with four different

Directors: (a) Director of stores, (b) Director of trade, (c) Director of textiles and (d) Director of farming, though the pivotal position had been given to the first one.

The Director of stores had been entrusted with covering the State requirements in goods, services and treasure. He exercised his control over the fields of agriculture, tax collections in towns and country, general commerce and barter, gifts in kind and grain, grain transactions, processing of food products, windfalls of revenue, general expenditure and also recovery of outstanding dues. Half of the stored products had to be kept for emergency reserves to meet times of scarcity while the other half had to be released for present consumption.

In his scheme of economic planning the concept of rationing had been introduced. Rations had been detailed for human beings and animals. The instruments used in weighing, grinding, pounding, winnowing of grains and other articles had also been mentioned.

Commerce which would, obviously, develop around such a pattern of commodity conservation, had to be supervised by a Director of trade. His supervision was over all merchandise flowing in through land and water routes and also over their respective prices. Market prices should be determined after centralizing the merchandise. Internal goods and royal commodities should have standardized markets while foreign goods must be dispersed. The people should sell both these goods in a manner to facilitate consumption. Exploitation either of markets or of consumers was not permitted. Besides, commodities in constant demand should have neither any restricted time of sale nor should be there any monopolistic practice.

Factory planning had been under the control of the Director of textiles. Here employment of workers was on social security basis. In specific processes of textile manufacturers there were widows, handicapped, destitute girls, old courtesans, palace maids, all of whom had been brought under social security. Wages had been adjusted to the quality of product turned out. For extra good work barter bonuses were to be paid. Expert weavers had also been employed and due stress on employer-employee good relations had been given.

Farm planning had been brought under the jurisdiction of Director of farming, whose functions covered all aspects of agriculture, horticulture, botanical sciences and arts. The Director should arrange for cultivation of State lands with the help of free and forced labour. The Director should arrange for farming implements. Meteorological forecasts helping farm operations should be properly serviced and farming processes adjusted accordingly. There should be facilities for the cultivation of uncultivated lands by granting concessions and subsidies. Cultivation under private irrigation should be encouraged by tax and cess exemption. Crop and product planning on different kinds of land had been described in detail. Similar had been the cultivation of medicinal herbs and plants. Farming wages had been indicated in produce according to work turned out. Grain collections had to be made as often as harvests were gathered.

Such short sketches of the various fields of economic activity covered by detailed planning as suggested by Kautilya give us a glimpse of the type of mono cyclical planning which he promulgated for strengthening the State so as to render it impregnable from within and invincible from without. The solitary idea dominating the entire structure of planning was loyalty to the State and loyalty to tradition.

e) ***Kautilya on Money***

Arthashastra by Kautilya is one of the major sources of information on the prevalence of ancient Indian coinage. In his treaties we can find some sporadic reference to the names of various coins in connection with reference to some fines and taxes. There is also the reference to counterfeit coins and espionage network for protection against it. Gold, silver and copper had been used for the manufacture of the coins. The superintendent of mint was entrusted with the task of minting coins while the inspector of coins was concerned with the task of testing of coins with regard to their weight and genuineness and the like.

An individual having some amount of gold and silver could have converted these into gold coin and silver coin respectively at the mint under the control of the State and for this the State could have charged a fee. For transaction purposes various denominations of coins had been used. Quite obviously, the restriction on the supply of money used to come from the availability of gold and silver.

f) ***Kautilya on Interest***

Kautilya had the clear prescription on the rate of interest and the method of recovery of debt. In this field, his idea was quite elaborate, complex and even modern. In this respect he had difference with his contemporary Aristotle, the Greek economist, who had considered charging interest on loans unjust. The two basic factors influencing the rate of interest were, according to Kautilya, the risk involved and the potential productivity of the money borrowed. Accordingly, he was in favour of introducing differential rate of interest. In his time, rate of interest had variation between 15 percent and 24 percent per annum. It may be mentioned here that the idea of expressing interest as a percent of so many units per hundred was in vogue in India.

The interest rate on secured loan for personal need for meeting matrimonial expenses was only 15 percent. However, interest on a loan taken for trade purposes was higher, for ordinary local trade the rate was 5 percent per month or 60 percent per annum while money borrowed for trading in forest product had simply got double the rate of interest. This is because the traders who used to travel forest areas had been subjected to greater risk from robbers and wild animals. Moreover, businesses in the periphery of forest had been more profitable. The rate of interest was maximum (240 percent per annum! almost unthinkable to us) for money borrowed for overseas trade as such a trade had been considered to be the most risky affair and at the same time most profitable too. Besides, the rate of interest was also high on loans borrowed by a group of people rather than by an individual in that the group would share the burden of interest and, naturally, it would not be burdensome on anyone individual. At the same time, the group was, generally, in a better position to pay high interest because it could be involved in large projects with greater potentiality of profits.

The creditors could not charge any interest they liked. But the interest rate to be charged by them must be approved by the State. Besides, there was the provision for some group of people being exempted from paying interest: students who were busy for making themselves ready for being good citizens, the bankrupt and sick who were unable to pay interest. Kautilya also advocated for different kinds of interest: compound interest, periodic interest, stipulated interest, daily interest and the use of a pledged article.

Summary and Conclusion

Judged by the foregoing analyses of Kautilya's various ideas related to money we are bewildered with the depth of his pragmatic philosophy underlying his work explicitly or implicitly expressed in *Arthashastra*. His idea of creating a Welfare State ascribing topmost priority to the people of the State is the symbol of nobleness pointed out as early as fourth century B.C. His concept of protecting young boys, women, elderly and the poverty-stricken indicates his mental agony for them. This statesman like economist cannot but be praised for being an ardent advocate of the introduction of social security measures for certain section of people of the country. At the same time he was strongly in support of keeping a vigil eye over the officials of the State. His great treaties are the first ever spelt out document about the principles of Public Finance in the framework of a decentralized administrative setup. His canons of taxation are still modern and we think that Kautilya might have sowed the seeds of Adam Smithian canons of taxation. He was a staunch supporter of surplus budget for the generation of which he had shown proper prescription.

Kautilya was in favour of introducing economic planning basically for the creation of wealth so that the strength of the State may be increased. For making it successful the responsibilities had been entrusted with four different Directors. In an agriculture-dominated economy he had, rightly, said that grain collection should be made as often as harvests get gathered. This principle is still in vogue in various parts of the globe.

His idea on money has given reference to different coins made of gold, silver and copper. His acute sense of reality inspired him to adopt proper guard against the counterfeit of the same. There have been numerous instances of the counterfeit of coins all over the world. The famous Tughlak king, Mohammad Bin Tughlak, for example, was puzzled at the introduction of copper coins during his regime. Had he listened to what had been in store in Arthashastra he could have easily avoided the untoward incident that befell him. Again, it is this counterfeit of coins that induced Sir Thomas Gresham (1519-1579), an English businessman and a public figure, to frame his famous law known as Gresham's Law. His treatment on differential rates of interest depending upon the risks involved and the potential productivity of the money borrowed brings out his acute sense of grim reality.

From the standpoint of the above considerations we may, unambiguously, state that some of the traits of modern economic thinking can be traced in the famous treatise of Kautilya. In the History of Economic Thought we owe much to Aristotle for being the earliest economic thinker. But our humble submission is that Kautilya, a very contemporary of Aristotle, should also be paid similar tribute. It is our firm conviction that many economic ideas developed after Kautilya have been, greatly, influenced by the economic ideas proclaimed by him and in this sense he can, really, be said to be a fore-runner of modern economic ideas. We can also conclude that Kautilya is great but re-discovered Kautilya is greater still.

REFERENCES

1. Basu, Ratanlal (2002): "Economic Aspects of Kautilya's Arthashastra—A Report on an International Symposium", *Artha Beekshan*, Vol. 11, No.1, June.
2. Bhatia, H. L. (1978): *History of Economic Thought*, Vikas Publishing House Pvt. Ltd., New Delhi.
3. Kangle, R. P. (1960): *Arthashastra*, Bombay: University of Bombay.
4. Ramaswamy, T. N. (1962): *Essentials of Indian Statecraft-Kautilya's Arthashastra for Contemporary Readers*, Asia Publishing House.
5. Sarkar, Sam (1999-2000): "Kautilyan Economics: An Analysis and Interpretation", *Indian Economic Journal*, Vol. 47, No.4.
6. Sen, Binoy C. (1967): *Economics in Kautilya, Research Series* 53, Sanskrit College, Kolkata.
7. Sen, Raj Kumar (2003): Globalization and Indian Economic Thinking in the Past and their Relevance in the present and future, Presidential Address, *86th Conference of the Indian Economic Association*, Shivaji University, Kolhapur, Maharashtra.

3

Corruption and Economic Growth in the Context of a Developing Economy

[Abstract

"Corruption", in the ordinary sense, means moral deterioration or "looseness of morals" or one of principles. He who indulges in bribery, dishonesty or abuse of public trusts without any scruple or qualm is said to be corrupted. Such a person may be a business man, a public official or a politician in power. The very common characteristic of each of these persons in different walks of life is that all of them generally try to serve their private interest by indulging in dishonest means. Thus corruption leads to illicit or under gains to some and losses to others.

Corruption stems from pervasive shortages. The problem of shortages is especially acute in a planned economy. The shortages are often deliberately created by bureaucrats in order to extort bribes from consumers. Corruption is, however, not a new term— it is as old as the civilization itself. The trace of corruption is found even in the writings of Kautilya in his famous treatise "Arthashastra". However, besides moral corruption, there are economic corruption and political corruption. Economic corruption itself can lead to political, legal and even moral corruption. Regarding political corruption the famous statesman Lord Linton said, "Power corrupts and absolute power corrupts absolutely."

There are two schools of thought regarding whether corruption leads to economic growth or not. One school of thought holds the view that in the context of pervasive and cumbersome regulations corruption may actually improve efficiency and thus helps economic growth. Another school of thought holds the view that with a corrupt bureaucracy in a regulatory regime a payment of bribes to get an investment license reduces the incentives to invest and thereby hampers economic growth.

It is a fact that corruption leads to lower economic growth as it seriously jeopardizes the incentives of the honest, sincere, laborious and diligent. Besides, it helps to concentrate income, real estate and wealth. This is undesirable, especially, in a developing economy. Hence whatever the effect of corruption in the economy may be, it should be eradicated tooth and nail.]

Introduction

There can be no denying the fact that the underdeveloped countries suffer from a lot of problems. One very acute problem of both developed and under developed countries is the prevalence of rampant corruption. India is not an exception to this common phenomenon. In India mild level of corruption started developing since the Second World War. However, it started to deteriorate since the beginning of the process of economic planning starting from April 1951, when public investment led to multiplier increase in income but the State took little step to distribute the income towards the goal of an egalitarian society as far as possible. The process of economic liberalization starting since July 1991 has brought in a plethora of scams in India and this has shaken violently the moral fabric of the Indian society. The sharp erosion in the role of the State to control the economy has enhanced and not reduced corruption as expected by the proponents of such policies. Its effect has been very precarious.

Meaning of Corruption

"*Corruption*", in the ordinary sense, means moral deterioration or "looseness of morals" or "looseness of principles". He who indulges in bribery, dishonesty or abuse of public trusts without any scruple or qualm is said to be corrupted. Such a person may be a businessman, a public official or a politician in power. The very common characteristic of each of these persons in different walks of life is that all of them generally try to serve their private interest by indulging in dishonest means. Thus corruption leads to illicit or under gains to some and losses to other.

Various attempts have been taken by different societies to make the people free from corruption. Thus religious preachings have been given, various moral and legal sanctions have been adopted and so on. In spite of that corruption could not be removed.

A Short History of Corruption

The word corruption is very often heard nowadays. Whenever we move from one place to another, we hear that we can not do any thing in this corrupt society. We also hear that corruption has reached to such an extent that with honesty almost nothing can be done. It is, as if, a new terminology. But this is not the reality. Corruption is as old as the civilization itself, though its degree has changed over time and it has developed from bad to worse. In fact, with the passage of time corruption instead of getting diminished, has been increasing. It may rightly be said that corruption, like leprosy and prostitution, is an ancient problem. We can find the trace of corruption even in the writings of Kautilya or Chanakya, the counselor and advisor to the noble king Chandra Gupta (reigning 321-297 B.C.). In his famous treatise "*Arthashastra*", Kautilya had stated, " Just as it is impossible not to taste the honey (or the poison) that find itself at the tip of the tongue, so it is impossible for a govt. servant not to eat up, at least a bit of the King's revenue. Just as fish moving under water can not possibly be found out either as drinking or not drinking water, so govt. servants employed in the govt. work can not be found out (while) taking money for themselves" (R.P. Kangle, 1972, p. 91). Kautilya mentions and comments on "forty ways of embezzlement". This being the case of corruption in India in the fourth century B.C., what the case of it may be in the twenty first century may be anybody's guess. In fact, there is rampant corruption in the far and wide of almost each and every country, developed and underdeveloped, of the world.

The Scottish man and philosopher-economist Adam Smith(1723-1790), the Father of Economics, observed in his very interesting treatise on a "*Theory of Moral Sentiments*", published before the *Wealth of Nations* (published in 1776 in two volumes) that morality is not born with us, but made by ourselves. Smith further observed in the last edition of the Sentiments with an uneasy awareness, according to a commentator, that the blandishment of a commercial society might prove too strong for the attainment of a high standard of virtue (p. 86). History is witness to the fact that corruption thrives mostly in an exchange economy established on the right of private property. The lure to acquire wealth by means of dishonesty can not but is great in an acquisitive society.

The assessment of Adam Smith regarding the root cause of corruption is absolutely correct when we go through his statement:

The disposition to admire and almost to worship, the rich and the powerful, and to despise, or at least to neglect persons of poor and mean condition—is, at the same time, the great and most universal cause of the corruption of our moral sentiments. That wealth and greatness are often regarded with respect and admiration which are due only to wisdom and virtue; and that vice and folly are the only proper objects, is often most unjustly bestowed upon poverty and weakness, has been the complaint of moralists of all ages.

The Practical Situation of Corruption and Sources of Corruption

In the ideal situation we desire both to be respectable and respected. Moreover, we dread both to be contemptible and to be condemned. However, upon coming into the world, we sooner or later find that wisdom and virtue are, by no means, the sole objects of respect and honor, nor is vice or folly or contempt. Every now and then we see the respectful attentions of the world to be more strongly directed towards the rich and the great than towards the wise and virtuous. In this regard there is a saying in Sanskrit whose English translation runs as "Even a person who is very miser, comes of an unerupted family and is shun by the honest people, is remembered and honored in the society if he has immense wealth." Off and on we see the vices and the follies of the powerful being much less despised than the poverty and weakness of the innocent. The great object of ambition and emulation in the world is to deserve, to acquire and to enjoy the respect, honor and admiration of mankind. To achieve this goal two different roads are presented before us: (1) by the study of wisdom and the practice of virtue and (2) by the acquisition of wealth and greatness. In this regard Adam Smith says:

"The wise and the virtuous, chiefly, a select, though I am afraid, but a small party who are the real and steady admirers or wisdom and virtue. The great mob of mankind are the admirers and worshippers, and what may seem more extraordinary, most frequently the disinterested admirers, of wealth and greatness" (*Sentiments*, p. 86).

From the previous practical scenario of human nature one question may reasonably arise in mind: If the seeds of corruption lie hidden in the very human nature itself, why is there lamentation over corruption? Is it not more practical to learn to live with corruption than to make vain efforts to root it out? From the stoic tolerance shown to corruption of every description in Indian society one may be tempted to draw the conclusion that most of the Indian people think in this way. But such an inference is absolutely false in as much as the Indian masses have so far not been equipped due to lack of literacy to deliberate on this very important social and moral question. Naturally, their acquisition to corruption is forced by ignorance and lack of power.

Sources of Corruption

Leaving apart moral corruption we may talk of two other varieties of corruption, namely (1) economic corruption and (2) political corruption.

In a simple word, it may be said that corruption stems from pervasive shortages. The problem of shortages is especially acute in a planned economy. The shortages are often deliberately created by bureaucrats in order to extort bribes from consumers.

Economic aspect of corruption is only one spearhead of this hydro-headed monster. Economic corruption can lead to political, legal and even moral corruption, bringing under its influence not only increasing resources but also increasing number of human beings. The situation is really critical when economic corruption is not considered as a crime but as a virtue of an intelligent and economically successful person.

Economic corruption, usually, refers to the use of public office for private gains. Of course, many other varieties of economic corruption are taking place everyday in the private sector. The bureaucrats having control over State resources, can easily profit from their position by threatening to deny access to such resources unless he is suitably bribed. Power can, thus, be lucrative to the corrupt. The businessman who overcharges for essential goods through creating an artificial scarcity by withholding supply at the ruling market price, the share market operators who corner equities in order to mislead the common investors for gain, the traders who practise over-invoicing of imports and undervoicing of exports, the tax dodgers, all indulge in corrupt practices that severely harm the society.

Economic corruption at the top is dangerous as it percolates to the bottom easily since masses try to follow the behavior of the elites. But corruption widespread at the bottom is more destructive for the whole society. In case we pay due attention to the practice of corruption by the common masses, the role of consumerism becomes significant.

Consumerism is a situation where due to technological advancement and commodity fetishism a multi-tier level of living is created in a society and due to revolution in transport system and communication, the demonstration effect becomes so strong as to induce people to aspire for reaching the higher level of living by fair means or foul. Since this process is constrained by income level, people try to shift their budget lines or the price lines continuously upwards, very often through unfair and illegal means as the scope for earning increasing amounts of white money is severely limited.

Again, since the marginal propensity to consume (MPC) of income earned through corruption is very high, the income and, consequently, consumption inequality increases sharply with the rise in relative poverty in a country like India , which is the habitant of the largest number of poor in the world. It may be stated that even in the 21st century about 25% of people of India live below the poverty line.

Let us now come to the idea of political corruption. In this regard, there is a famous statement made by Lord Linton: "Power corrupts and absolute power corrupts absolutely." That this is a fact can be realized if we minutely look at the present scenario of the world power.

It may be said that political corruption takes place when the ill-gotten gains obtained through dishonesty are basically in terms of political power. Long stay in the government by a particular political party, very low strength of opposition in the government, dictatorship, very good organization at the grassroots level, unconsciousness of the masses over the present political scenario, satisfying behavior of the masses with little attainment, intimidation of the persons in power on any opposition, the policy of destroying something upon the inefficient person, continuous amelioration of the party in power by hook or by crook, incessant allure of persons belonging to other parties towards the party in power and so on are sowing the seeds of political power.

Coming to the scenario of India we may say that some sort of a patron-client relationship between bureaucrats, politicians and business has been obtained since the attainment of political independence on 15th August, 1947. According to many, most of the economic corruption in our country has originated from this very source alone.

Corruption and Economic Growth

Economic growth is defined as a rate of expansion that makes an underdeveloped country move from a near subsistence mode of living to a substantially higher level of living in a comparatively short period of time, in decades rather than in centuries. The basic indicator of economic growth is a rise in per capita product. Bearing this definition of economic growth in mind, let us now see whether corruption can lead to economic growth or not.

In this respect there are two schools of opinion. One school of opinion holds the view that in the context of pervasive and cumbersome regulations, especially in the context of developing countries in the world, corruption may actually improve efficiency and thus help economic growth. Nathaniel H. Leff opines, "If the government has erred in its decision, the course made possible by corruption may well be the better one." Also to many non-economists corruption is the much-desired grease for a rigid administration. Samuel P. Huntington clearly advocates, "In terms of economic growth the only thing worse than a society with a rigid, over-centralized dishonest bureaucracy is one with a rigid, over-centralized honest bureaucracy."

The fundamental idea of this school of thought seems to be growth at any cost. It may be stated that while a rigid bureaucracy may put hurdles on the path of growth, we do not think that the best available way to overcome these difficulties is corruption. Corruption tends to undermine the fear of law, in general, in public mind and hence strikes out at the very foundation of a democratic society.

According to another school of thought, corruption does, actually, harm economic growth of a country. The opinion of this school of thought may be put in the following manner.

With a corrupt bureaucracy in a regulatory regime a payment of bribes to get an investment license, definitely, reduces the incentive to invest even apart from affecting the composition of investment. In the taxation system of many a country in the world, negative profits (that is, losses) can be deducted from taxable investment income but bribes can not be shown as losses for calculation of tax liability. This is, particularly, harmful for risk-taking in the context of innovation. Similarly, the moment public resources meant for building productivity-enhancing infrastructure are diverted for private consumption of the bureaucrats or politicians or businessmen (for instance, cement and steel for public goods or dams used for luxury homes and the like), growth process will, obviously, be adversely affected.

Another growth effect follows from the fact that higher bribes result in declining profitability on productive investments relative to speculative investments. Some of these growth effects have, statistically, been corroborated from cross-country data.

Corrupt bureaucrats in less developed countries may opt for import of complex technology or goods (where detecting proper valuation or over-invoicing is more difficult) in preference to more standardized but possibly more appropriate technology or goods.

Pranab Bardhan states, "For similar reason, allocating government funds in a few large defense contracts may look more attractive to the officials involved than spending the money in building numerous small rural health clinics". To preserve the secrecy of deals a small elite group may also try to raise entry barriers for outsiders, which, in many situations, has the effect of discouraging the flow of new ideas and innovations. Secret payments, particularly by foreign companies, also tend to be accumulated and spent not inside the country but abroad.

Finally, in case there is rampant corruption, traditional values, religious sanctions and honest sermon against corruption break down. Such a situation thus makes corruption universal and this, ultimately, leads to lower economic growth.

Anti-corruption Policies Recommended

It is a fact that corruption leads to lower economic growth as it seriously jeopardizes the incentives of honest, sincere, laborious and diligent. Besides, corruption helps to concentrate income, real estate and wealth. This is undesirable, especially, in a developing country. Hence we want to prescribe some anti-corruption policies:

1. To reduce bureaucratic corruption, the monopoly power of the bureaucrats when a client faces him/her in trying to get a license or some subsidy or transfer, should be ended. In the opinion of the experts instead of giving each official a clearly defined sphere of influence over which he/she has monopoly power, they should be given competing jurisdictions so that a client, not being well- served by one official, may move to another. In case collusion among several officials becomes difficult, severe competition could tend to drive the level of bribes to zero.

2. An incentive pay structure for public officials has been considered by many as the most effective means to fight corruption. We may cite the cases of Hong Kong and Singapore, the two Asian tigers, both of which have, in recent years, followed an incentive wage policies for public officials. Both the countries have attained a good deal of success in this respect.

3. A very important source of corruption, in a political democracy, is to dispense favours for campaign contributions. Since elections are highly expensive, large campaign contributions are essential for success in them. This is true irrespective of the nature of the country concerned having elected govt. In such a

situation what is important to fight political corruption is to institutionalize different kinds of accountability mechanisms, namely (i) an election commission to limit and enforce rules on campaign contributions, (ii) an independent office of public auditing, (iii) in democratic elections independent investigation agencies (for example, the Hong Kong Independent Committee against corruption which directly reports to the Governor General), (iv) an office of local ombudsman with some control over the bureaucracy, (v) citizens' watch-dog committees providing information and monitoring services and pursuing public interest litigation, (vi) a rigorous and independent, even muckraking press, (vii) less stringent libel laws or laws protecting official secrecy.

Conclusion

In conclusion, we would like to say that however effective such an anti-corruption policy may be, neither removing nor rooting out corruption is possible in the so-called, Adam Smith's "Commercial Society", that is, in a free market economy.

The only silver lining in this current gloomy situation is the international concern about the economic cost of corruption, especially in countries where perception of corruption is quite high. Unfortunately, our country, India, has been rated among the twenty most corrupted countries in the world. A few years ago twenty nine OECD and five other countries signed a convention banning bribery of foreign public officials in international business transactions. This will, it is expected, reduce the flow of money meant for corruption to low-income countries.

In India, the situation prevailing at present calls for reprioritization of government intervention in the desired directions. A broad-based labour-intensive growth can help our country to reduce income inequality and a transfer of resources to the production of goods for mass consumption can reduce both absolute and relative poverty. This can, in fine, bring down economic corruption to the tolerable limit.

REFERENCES

1. Ackley, G: *Macroeconomic Theory.*
2. Bardhan, Pranab (1997):"Corruption and Development: A Review of Issues", *Journal of Economic Literature*, September.
3. Brademas, John and Heimann, Fritz (1988): Tackling International Corruption: No Longer Taboo, *Foreign Affairs*, September\October.
4. Datt, Ruddar and Sundharam, K.P.M.(2006): *Indian Economy*, S. Chand & Company Ltd, New Delhi.
5. Huntington, Samuel P. (1968): *Political Order in Changing Societies*, New Haven, Yale University Press.
6. Kangle, R.P. (1972): *The Kautilya Arthasastra*, Part-2, University of Bombay.
7. Klitgaard, Robert(1998): International Co-operation Against Corruption, *Finance & Development*, March.
8. Konar, D.N. (2005): "Economic Ideas of Koutilya", *Economic Affairs*, Vol. 50, Qrt, March.
9. Nathaniel h. Leff(1964): "Economic Development Through Bureaucratic Corruption", *The American Behavioral Scientist*, November.
10. Mauro, Paolo (I998): "Corruption: Causes, Consequences and Agenda for Further Research", *Finance & Development*, March.
11. Seminar on "*Corruption and Development" Organized by the Department of Economics*, Rabindra Bharati University, Kolkata on 12.03.1999.
12. Sen, Raj Kumar (1988): "Planning for Indian Economic Development", *Economic Growth and Social Change*, March.

13. Sen, Raj Kumar (1982): "Parallel Economy and Economic Dualism in India", *Indian Economic Association*, Conference Volume, Jabalpur.
14. Shelly, Loussel (1998): " Crime and Corruption in the Digital Age", *Journal of International Affairs*, Spring.
15. Smith, Adam: *A Theory of Moral Sentiments*.
16. Organization for Economic Co-operation and Development (OECD) (1999), Nations get tough on Sleazy Multinational Corporations, *The Economic Times*, February 16.

4

Women's Role in the Present High Rate of Population Growth in India

[Abstract

Women in many highly populated countries of the world may play a very significant role in quickly arresting the present high growth of population. This is, especially, true to India where between 1951 and 2001 population increased at an annual compound rate of 2.36 percent. The high rate of growth of population that our country has been facing, has been eating into the vitality of our country and it has created a stumbling block on the path of development of the Indian Economy. What we need is, thus, the quick arrest of the growth of population. In this context the women, in general, and educated women, in particular, can play a very vital role.

It is a fact that a healthy society will have lower rate of growth of population. Good health of a society is measured, among other things, by a lower infant mortality rate and high expectation of life at birth. Both these demographic variables are highly correlated, especially, with the female literacy rates.

Besides, the growth rate of population can be controlled, to a significant extent, if the fertility rate can be checked. One way of materializing this is the dissemination of education, especially, among women. It has also been noticed that TFR is an inverse function of the level education of the mothers.

High literacy rate leads to lowering IMR and it also enhances ELB. Lower IMR and high ELB lead to a lower birth rate which will lead to a fall in the level of poverty and that will also reduce the problem of child labour to a good extent. A society where IMR declines, ELB increases, poverty diminishes and child labour disappears, can not but approach to a developed society.]

Introduction

The purpose of the present article is to show that women in many highly populated countries of the world can play a very significant role in quickly arresting the present high growth of population. This is, especially, true to India where between 1951 and 2001 population increased at an annual compound rate of 2.36 percent. Today, India with an area of about 2.36 percent of the world, has been nourishing about 17 percent population of the world. Three of our metropolitan cities, namely Mumbai, Kolkata and Delhi with respective population of 16.5, 13.3 and 13.0 million got the fifth, the seventh and the ninth rank respectively in 2001 in the list of seventeen mega cities of the world, each having a population of at least ten million.

The high rate of growth of population of our country has been eating into the vitality of our country and it has created a stumbling block on the path of development of the Indian economy. The high rate of growth of population with the consequent result of huge unemployment has almost crippled our economy. What is needed is, therefore, the quick arrest of the growth of population. It is in this context that the women, in general, and educated women, in particular, can play a very vital role.

Data and Methodology

To substantiate the stated objective we have taken some demographic information on a number of aspects of fifteen major States of India. By major States we have meant those States whose population, according to 1991 census, was at least ten million. These States, in alphabetical order, are: Andhra Pradesh, Assam, Bihar, Gujarat, Haryana, Karnataka, Kerala, Madhya Pradesh, Maharashtra, Orissa, Punjab, Rajasthan, Tamil Nadu, Uttar Pradesh and West Bengal. The demographic information are basically on: (1) Female Literacy Rates (FLR), (2) Infant Mortality Rates (IMR), (3) Crude Birth Rate (CBR), (4) Crude Death Rate (CDR), (5) Expectation of Life at Birth (ELB), (6) General Fertility Rate (GFR) and (7)Total Fertility Rate (TFR). Besides, there are (8) Per Capita Income at current prices (PCY) and (9) Human Development Index (HDI). The per capita income at current prices will indicate the material position of the States concerned. All data relating to these demographic features are secondary data which are available from various reports of the Government of India; the Economic Survey, the Government of India, 2005-06; the various publications of the Bureau of Applied Economics and Statistics, Government of West Bengal; Sample Registration System—Statistical Report 2001; Sample Registration System—Analytical Studies Report No.1 of 2006; Sample Registration System—Special Fertility & Mortality Survey 1998, various statements and the like. The information on per capita income at current prices has been taken from Statistical Outline of India, various issues, Tata Services Limited.

The available data have been put in the appropriate Tables and usual ranks ranging from 1 to 15 have been ascribed to the already-mentioned fifteen major States. In case there has been any tie, the normal statistical procedure for allotting the appropriate rank has been adhered to. We have calculated Spearman's rank correlation coefficient between a number of two related series of demographic variables such as (1) FLR and IMR, (2) FLR and ELB, (3) FLR and CBR, (4) FLR and GFR, (5) FLR and TFR, (6) CBR and IMR, (7) CBR and ELB and (8) CDR and IMR. Besides, there is the rank correlation coefficient between FLR and PCY of the States and that between FLR and HDI. The data on demographic variables relate basically to the census years 1991 and 2001.

Relation between Spread of Education among Women and Good Health

Good health of a society is measured, among other things, by a lower infant mortality rate and high expectation of life at birth. Both these demographic variables are highly correlated, especially with the female literacy rates. Column(2) of Table4.1 displays the census figures of the female literacy rates in 2001 while columns (3), (4) and (5) portray the information on CDR in 2003, IMR in 2002 and ELB during 1998-2002 respectively. Both figures of columns (4) and (5) have been taken from Economic Survey, 2005-06, Government of India. The information on CDR has also been taken from this source.

From Table 4.1 we notice that about 88 percent of women in Kerala are literate while only 33.6 percent of Bihari women are literate. In case of West Bengal this percentage is a little more than 60. Coming to IMR it is seen that in case of Kerala this rate is just 10 while in Orissa this is 87 and in Madhya Pradesh this is 85. In Tamil Nadu this is 44 and in West Bengal this is 49. Again, Kerala attaining an ELB of 73.5 years has topped the list of Indian States while Punjab with an ELB of 68.5 years has got the second rank and Maharashtra with an ELB of 66.2 years has occupied the third place.

Table 4.1

Information on FLR, CDR, IMR and ELB of the Fifteen Major States of India and Ranks Attained by them*

Major States of India	*FLR in 2001 (ranks in descending order)*	*Crude Death Rate per 1000 in 2003 (ranks in ascending order)*	*Infant Mortality Rate, 2002 (ranks in ascending order)*	*ELB, 1998-2002 (ranks in descending order)*
Andhra Pradesh	51.2 (10)	8.0 (11)	62(9.5)	63.5(8)
Assam	56.0(9)	9.1 (12)	70(11)	57.9(14)
Bihar	33.6(15)	7.9(10)	61(8)	60.8(11)
Gujarat	58.6(6)	7.6(8)	60(7)	63.4(9)
Haryana	56.3(8)	7.1(4)	62 (9.5)	65.2(4.5)
Karnataka	57.5(7)	7.2(5.5)	55(6)	64.5(6)
Kerala	87.9(1)	6.3(1)	10(1)	73.5(1)
Madhya Pradesh	50.3(12)	9.8 (15)	85(14)	56.9(15)
Maharashtra	67.5(2)	7.2(5.5)	45(3)	66.2(3)
Orissa	51.0(1)	9.7(14)	87(15)	58.5(13)
Punjab	63.6(4)	7.0(3)	51(5)	68.5(2)
Rajasthan	44.3(13)	7.6(8)	78(12)	61.1(10)
Tamil Nadu	64.6(3)	7.6(8)	44(2)	65.2(4.5)
Uttar Pradesh	43.0(14)	9.5(13)	80(13)	59.1(12)
West Bengal	60.2(5)	6.6(2)	49(4)	63.9(7)
All-India	54.3	8.0	63	62.5

Source: Economic Survey, Government of India, 2005-06 and Census of India, 2001.

* Figures within parentheses indicate the ranks attained by the States.

The rank correlation coefficient between FLR and IMR has been calculated to be +0.85, signifying that higher the literacy rate among females in a State lower is the IMR in that State. Again, the rank correlation coefficient between FLR and ELB has been found to be +0.81. That is, ELB has been observed to be highly correlated with the FLR. This also means that the higher the literacy rate among females the higher is the ELB.

Relation between Spread of Education among Women and Fertility Rates

It is known to all that India is the second most populous country in the world. According to the latest census of 2001, our population is 1020 million and we are very much in need of arresting the present trend of the growth rate of population, lest a catastrophe befalls us any time. The growth rate of population can be controlled to a significant extent if the fertility rate can be checked. One way of doing this is the dissemination of education, especially among women. This has been shown by the calculated values of the rank correlation coefficients computed from various information presented in Table 4.2.

We see from Table 4.2 that in respect of CBR, GFR and TFR Kerala has attained the top rank and Tamil Nadu, following Kerala, has attained the second rank. While the position of these two States has been unique, no conclusive statement can be made with respect to other States. With regard to the rank correlation coefficients we have seen that this between FLR and CBR has been as high as +0.90. This high value of the coefficient of correlation suggests that with the dissemination of education among women the birth rate starts declining. Again, with the spread of education among women the general fertility rate starts declining. This has been established by the fact that the rank correlation coefficient between FLR in 2001 and GFR in 2000-02 has been found to be +0.84. Moreover, with the expansion of education TFR also goes on declining. This has been demonstrated by the fact that the rank correlation coefficient between FLR in 2001 and TFR in the same year has been found to be +0.83.

Table 4.2
Information on CBR, GFR and TFR in Respect of Fifteen Major States of India and the Ranks Attained by Them*

Major States of India	*CBR (per 1000) in 2003 (ranks in ascending order)*	*GFR in 2000-02 (per 1000) ranks in ascending order*	*TFR in 2001 (ranks in ascending order*
Andhra Pradesh	20.4(5)	78.0(4)	2.3(3)
Assam	26.3(10.5)	100.9(10)	3.0(10)
Bihar	30.7(4)	133.8(14)	4.4(14)
Gujarat	24.6(9)	94.3(9)	2.9(9)
Haryana	26.3(10.5)	106.5(11)	3.1(11)
Karnataka	21.8(7)	80.3(7)	2.4(5.5)
Kerala	16.7(1)	59.5(1)	1.8(1)
Madhya Pradesh	30.2(12)	128.1(12)	3.9(12)
Maharashtra	19.9 (3)	80.0(6)	2.4(5.5)
Orissa	23.0 (8)	89.0 (8)	2.6(8)
Punjab	20.6 (6)	79.9 (5)	2.4(5.5)
Rajasthan	30.3 (13)	129.0 (13)	4.0(13)
Tamil Nadu	18.3 (2)	67.8 (2)	2.0(2)
Uttar Pradesh	31.3 (15)	140.3 (15)	4.5(15)
West Bengal	20.3 (14)	76.8(3)	2.4(5.5)
All-India	24.8	99.8	–

Source: Economic Survey, 2005-06, Government of India.

* Figures within parentheses indicate ranks attained by the States.

Relation between Spread of Education among Women and Development

We know that economic development is a process whereby the per capita real income of a nation increases over a long period of time. There are a number of indicators of economic development. One such indicator is the increase in per capita income. It has been seen that the spread of education among women and per capita income are highly positively correlated. This implies that with the expansion of education among women, per capita income also goes on expanding. The per capita income at current prices in 1990-91 and 2000-01 of the States dealt with here has been presented in Table 4.3.

Table 4.3

Per Capita Income of the Fifteen Major States of India at Current Prices and Ranks Attained by Them *

Major States of India	*Per Capita Income (Rs.) at current prices in 1990-91 (ranks in descending order)*	*Per Capita Income (Rs.) at current prices in 2000-01 (ranks in descending order)*
Andhra Pradesh	4816 (10)	16373 (8)
Assam	4432 (12)	11357 (11)
Bihar	2966 (15)	5466 (15)
Gujarat	6343 (4)	19228 (6)
Haryana	7721 (2)	23742 (2)
Karnataka	4975 (8)	18041 (7)
Kerala	5110 (6)	21310 (4)
Madhya Pradesh	4798 (11)	10803 (12)
Maharashtra	7612 (3)	23726 (3)
Orissa	3166 (14)	8547 (14)
Punjab	8177 (1)	25048 (1)
Rajasthan	4883 (9)	13116 (10)
Tamil Nadu	5541 (5)	20975 (5)
Uttar Pradesh	3937 (13)	9721 (13)
West Bengal	5072(7)	16072 (9)

Source: Statistical Outline of India, 2002-03 and 2003-04, Tata Services Limited, Department of Economics and Statistics, Bombay House, Mumbai.

*Figures within parentheses indicate rank.

Table 4.3 displays that in respect of per capita income at current prices in both 1990-91 and 2000-01, Punjab has headed the list of States analyzed here while the second place in both the years has been captured by Haryana. In this field the third and the fifth rank have gone to Maharashtra and Tamil Nadu respectively. It may be mentioned that though Punjab and Haryana have not attracted us much in respect of some of the vital statistics dealt with here, these two States have excelled in the field of per capita income. We have calculated the rank correlation coefficient between FLR in 1991 and per capita income at current prices in 1990-91 and seen that this correlation has assumed the value of +0.71. However, the same coefficient, after a decade, has been found to be +0.82, quite a high value. Thus more spread of education among women has led to more per capita income. Obviously, more per capita income may mean more development. It is interesting to note that the rank correlation coefficient between per capita income at current prices among the fifteen States in 1990-91 and 2000-01 has been as high as +0.96, that is, almost perfect. This reveals that with respect to the per capita income at current prices the ranking of the major States in 1990-91 and 2000-01 has remained almost unaltered.

Relation between Spread of Education among Women and Human Development

We know that over the last twenty years or so a significant emphasis in economic literature has been put on various aspects of human development. The pioneers in this field are experts of the United Nations Development' Programme (UNDP), mainly late Dr. Mahbub-ul-Haq and Professor Amartya Sen. It has been seen that the female literacy rate and the human development index are highly positively correlated. For this we have inserted Table 4.4 which contains besides human development index in 1991, FLR and GFR in 1991.

Table 4.4
FLR, HDI and GFR of Fifteen Major States of India in 1991 and Ranks Attained by Them*

Major States of India	*FLR in 1991 (ranks in descending order)*	*HDI in 1991 (ranks in ascending order)*	*GFR (per 1000) in 1991 (ranks in ascending order)*
Andhra Pradesh	32.7(11)	0.344(9)	101.2(3)
Assam	43.0 (8)	0.326 (11)	117.9(10)
Bihar	22.9(14)	0.286 (13)	140.1(12)
Gujarat	48.6(5)	0.380.(6)	111.3(9)
Haryana	40.5(9)	0.409(4)	136.1(11)
Karnataka	44.3(7)	0.367(8)	105.4(5)
Kerala	86.2(1)	0.576(1)	65.4(1)
Madhya Pradesh	28.8(12)	0.282.(15)	151.8(14)
Maharashtra	52.3(2)	0.403(5)	104.9(4)
Orissa	34.7(10)	0.328(10)	110.8(7.5)
Punjab	50.4(4)	0.447(2)	110.8(7.5)
Rajasthan	20.4(15)	0.298 (12)	147.8(13)
Tamil Nadu	51.3(3)	0.421(3)	78.4(2)
Uttar Pradesh	25.3(13)	0.284(14)	158.9(15)
West Bengal	46.6(6)	0.370(7)	106.0(6)
All-India	39.3	0.340	120.6

Source: Census of India, 1991 and National Human Development Report, 2001

* Figures within parentheses indicate ranks attained by the States.

It is interesting to note that the rank correlation coefficient of FLR in 1991 and 2001 has been +0.98, that is, almost perfect. This implies that with respect to the FLR among major States in India the ranking of the States has remained almost unaltered. Again, the rank correlation coefficient between FLR in 1991 and GFR in 1991 has been calculated to be +0.77 (Table 4.4) while that between the same two variables a decade later was +0.84 (videTable 4.1 and 4.2). Thus for getting a better human development index more expansion of literacy among women is urgently called for and also for reducing the GFR more advancement of FLR is of utmost necessity.

Advancement of Literacy Rate among Women and the Consequent Fall in GFR in 2001

A minute look at the second column of Table 4.1 and that very column of Table 4.4 reveals that in comparison to 1991 each and every major State of India discussed here has seen a positive percentage change in the female literacy rate while with respect to the figures of the general fertility rate (column 4 of Table 4.4 and column 3 of Table 4.2) each and every State has seen a negative percentage change. This is tantamount to saying that an advancement of the female literacy rate has caused a fall in the GFR. Coming to the all-India scenario we see that there has been 37.9 percent change (increase) in the female literacy rate between 1991 and 2001 while there has been 17.2 percent change (decrease) in the GFR between the same period. This amounts to saying that about 38 percent increase in the FLR has produced more than 17 percent fall in the GFR at the all-India level.

Looking at the performance of the individual States we cannot, however, come to a definite conclusion. In case of Kerala only 4.3 percent increase in FLR has been accompanied with about 24 percent fall in GFR and in case of Bihar even about 47 percent increase in FLR has caused only 4.5 percent fall in GFR. In case of Madhya Pradesh about 75 percent enhancement of FLR has produced about 16 percent fall in GFR whereas in West Bengal about 29 percent increase in FLR has caused about 28 percent fall in GFR. In Punjab about 26 percent advancement in FLR has produced about 28 percent fall in GFR and in Orissa 47 percent increase in FLR has produced about 20 percent fall in GFR. Thus barring the so-called BIMARU States, all major States of India have been able to produce a very strong impact on the GFR consequent upon an advancement of the FLR. This encourages us to state that in order to reduce the GFR we are urgently in need of enhancing the literacy rate among females.

It may be added here that the rank correlation coefficient between FLR in 1991 and GFR in 1991 was +0.77 while the same coefficient in 2001 (that is, after the gap of ten years when there was more progress in FLR in each and every State) improved to +0.84 . That is, with the passage of time we find a stronger relationship between FLR and GFR .

Level of Education of Mothers and Total Fertility Rates in India

The level of education of mothers is itself a vital determinant of total fertility rate in a country, especially in a developing one. The information portrayed in Table 4.5 will highlight this fact.

Table 4.5
Total Fertility Rate in India by Level of Education of Mothers in 2001

Level of Education of Mothers	Total Fertility Rate		
	Total	*Rural*	*Urban*
(a) Illiterate	4.1	4.3	3.2
(b) Literate	2.4	2.6	2.2
(c) Without any formal education	3.9	4.0	3.4
(d) Below primary	3.5	3.6	2.9
(e) Primary	2.3	2.4	2.1
(f) Middle	2.0	2.0	2.0
(g) Class X	1.8	1.9	1.8
(h) Class XII	1.5	1.5	1.5
(i) Graduate and above	1.5	1.4	1.5
Aggregate	3.1	3.4	2.3

Source: Sample Registration System, Statistical Report, 2001, Report No.1 of 2004, Office of the Registrar General, India.

What the above Table suggests is that TFR is an inverse function of the level of education of mothers. This means that with the increase in the educational level of mothers there appears a quick fall in the TFR. This comes to be true till the attainment of education up to class XII standard.

Summary of the Analysis

The basic reasons behind the high growth rate of population in India can, clearly, be understood if we minutely look at the behaviour of the CBR, CDR and IMR across the major States of India as portrayed in Tables 4.1 and 4.2. Table 4.2 discloses that the all-India average birth rate in 2003 was 24.8 per 1000 persons and only six States, namely Haryana, Assam, Rajasthan, Madhya Pradesh, Bihar and Uttar Pradesh (that is, Haryana and Assam, besides the BIMARU States) had birth rates higher than this average. We get perplexed by noting that Haryana, possessing the second place in India in terms of per capita income at current prices in 2000-01, has not yet been in a position to reduce the birth rate to a significant extent. In this respect the success of the States occupying the first nine ranks where the birth rate is less than 25 is really creditable. Other States should emulate their example.

The all-India average death rate in 2003 was 8.0 per 1000 persons, which is quite satisfactory. In this respect the performance of all the States barring Assam, Uttar Pradesh, Orissa and Madhya Pradesh is quite good. (In this respect Bihar just lies on the border). Coming to the trend of the IMR which is a very good indicator of health and economic development of a country, we note that the all-India figure in this rate in 2002 was 63 which is relatively high when we compare this figure with those attained by many developed countries of the world. In this sphere we cannot but praise the success achieved by Kerala. Tamil Nadu, Maharashtra, West Bengal, Punjab, Karnataka and Gujarat had also made commendable success in this affair. However, the achievement by States like Orissa, Madhya Pradesh, Uttar Pradesh, Rajasthan and Assam is really very dismal.

We have calculated the Spearman's rank correlation coefficient between CBR and IMR and also that between CDR and IMR after attaching ranks attained by the above-mentioned States in these three aspects in the usual manner (vide Tables 4.1 and 4.2). The former has been found to be +0.78 while the latter one has been as high as +O.81.It is likely that the States having high (low) IMR will have high(low)death rate and our study also corroborates this finding. The birth rate is also highly correlated with the IMR. Hence one way of reducing birth rate to a significant extent is to have a spectacular reduction in the IMR as has been done by Kerala occupying the first rank in respect of each of the demographic features presented in various Tables. If the parents get assured that their new-born will survive, they will, in general, not hesitate to adopt family planning scheme. However, if they are not sure of the survival of their new child, they will, unhesitatingly, not adopt the family planning scheme.

Conclusion

Higher literacy rate, especially among women, leads to lowering IMR and that also enhances life expectancy at birth. Lower IMR and higher ELB lead to a lower birth rate. A high value of IMR is one of the fundamental reasons behind high growth rate of population of our country. Hence to control high growth rate of population the IMR should be brought to the minimum. The IMR has been found to be highly correlated with the literacy rate of women. Therefore, if literacy can be spread among almost hundred per cent females, not only the IMR can be brought to the minimum but also the rate of growth of population can be reduced to a good extent.

Again, higher literacy rate among women leads to lower TFR and that will, again, lead to a fall in birth rate. A lower birth rate will lead to a fall in the level of poverty and that will also reduce the problem of child labour.

A society where the IMR declines, ELB increases, poverty diminishes and child labour disappears, cannot but approach to a developed society.

REFERENCES

1. *Economic Review, Government of West Bengal,* Relevant Issues.
2. *Economic Survey,* Government of India, 2005-06.
3. Konar, D.N. (1989): "Role of Education in Reducing the Growth of Population in India", *Artha Shastra,* Vol. 8, No.2.
4. Konar, D.N. (2004): *The Scenario of Population Growth in India,* Akansha Publishing House, New Delhi.
5. Konar, D.N. (2006):The Behaviour of Infant Mortality Across the Districts of West Bengal", Business Insight, *Journal of the Department of Commerce,* Burdwan University, Vol. 1, No.1.
6. Konar, D.N. (2007): "Women and the Present High Rate of Population Growth in India", *Artha Beekshan,* Vol. 16, No. 1 June.
7. NFHS-2, West Bengal, *National Family Health Survey India, 1998-99,* International Institute for Population Sciences, Mumbai, October, 2001.
8. Roy, Sachchidananda (2002): Manab Unnayan: Paschim Banger Jela Chitra, *Seriba,* South-24 Parganas.
9. Sample Registration System, *Statistical Reports 1998, 2001, 2002 and 2004,* Office of the Registrar General, India.
10. *Statistical Outline of India, 2002-03 and 2003-04,* Tata Services Limited, Department of Economics and Statistics, Bombay House, Mumbai 400001.

5

Trend of Indian Agriculture in the Post-Independence Period

[Abstract

India is still now an agriculture-based economy and it pertinently holds a very important place in our National Economy. It is the mainstay of the vast majority of the population of the country. Even today, 58 percent of the working population of the country remains in the field of agriculture. Still now it accounts for about 22 percent of the GDP and it still provides maximum employment to our ever-increasing labor force. However, in the first half of the last century annual compound growth rate of agriculture was only 0.3 percent while in the second half of that century this growth rate jumped to around 3 percent.

The Green Revolution in the field of agriculture in the late sixties of the last century had brought a significant change in the sphere of productivity and production of major agricultural crops. The growth rate of agriculture became so high that it outstripped the annual growth rate of population of the country.

However, Indian agriculture fared badly during the reform period when output of most of the agricultural crops became significantly lower than what it was attained earlier. This is, especially, true to wheat, pulses, oil-seeds and the like. As a consequence, supply of these products became less than the corresponding demand for these. The Planning Commission has taken note of it and is very eager for bringing back the golden days of Indian agriculture. We only hope that its trial will be fruitful in the 11th Five Year Plan.]

Introduction

There can be no denying the fact that India is basically a land of agriculture as it pertinently holds a very important place in our National Economy. It is the mainstay of the vast majority of our population. Even today more than 58 per cent of our working population remains in the field of agriculture (Economic Survey, 2003-04). Still now agriculture accounts for about 22 per cent of our Gross Domestic Product (GDP) and it still provides maximum employment to our ever increasing labor force. It has been known that even now 72 per cent of our population lives in rural areas (Census of India, 2001) spreading over six lakh of villages. A very imporant aspect of Indian Economy is with regard to the percentage of total workers engaged in agriculture mainly as cultivators and agricultural laborers, comprising about 50 per cent of total work force of India, according to the latest census of 2001.

In the light of this we intend to investigate into the trend of Indian agriculture for a long period of 56 years from 1950-51 to 2006-07. This has been done in different phases:

Phase 1: From 1950-51 to 1985-86 divided into two parts:

(a) From 1950-51 to 1964-65

(b) From1965-66 to 1985-86

Phase 2: From 1950-51 to 1992-93

Phase 3: From 1980-81 to 1989-90

Phase 4: From 1990-91 to 2000-01

Phase 5: From 2000-01 to 2006-07.

This being the sequence of our study of the Indian agriculture, we shall give more attention to Phase 1.

Trend of Indian Agriculture Between 1950-51 and 1985-86

Purpose and Methodlogy

The purpose of this chapter is to examine whether a breakthrough in our agriculture has been attained after the introduction of high yielding variety (HYV) technology in the mid-sixties. This will be examined by fitting three growth curves[(a)], namely

(1) Linear $Y_t=a+bt$,

(2) Exponential $Y_t=ab^t$ and

(3) Gompertz $Y_t=ab^{c^t}$,

a,b and c being the parameters.

The point as well as trend rates of growth can be estimated by using the fitted curve.

For (1) the point rate of growth is a decreasing function of time and the trend rate of growth is zero whereas for (2) both are constant. For (3), however, the point and trend rates of growth depend upon the magnitudes of the parameters, b and c. If both b and c assume values greater than one, the point growth rate will be an increasing function of time and the trend rate of growth is infinity. If, on the other hand, they are less than one, the point rate of growth will be a decreasing function of time and the trend rate of growth will be zero.

The goodness of fit among the competing growth curves has been examined by the 'D' value defined as

$D = \frac{\Sigma_t (y_t - Y_t)^2}{\Sigma (y_t - \bar{y})^2}$ where Y_t is the estimated value while y_t is the actual value.

Since $D = 1 - r^2$ (r^2 being the simple coefficient of determination) the smaller the value of D, the larger will be the value of r^2, that is, the larger will be the value of ryY, that is, the simple coefficient of correlation between the actual values (y) and the corresponding estimated values (Y) of the relevant variable. So out of three alternative forms of curves that giving the least value of D will be the best fitting and the magnitude of parameters (b and c) of such a curve will be either the trend growth rate [for (2)] or the direction of the point growth rates [for (1) and (3)].

The above–mentioned three curves have been fitted to production (P), yield (Y) and acreage (A) under cultivation of some major crops produced in India. This has been covered in two different types of analysis: (a) Aggregative Analysis and (b) Disaggregative Analysis. In the former case we have concentrated upon three groups of crops viz., (i) food crops, (ii) non-food crops and (iii) all crops, while in the latter category our discussion has been extended to thirteen individual crops, namely Rice, Wheat, Jawar, Bajra, Maize, Gram, Total Pulses, Potatoes, Jute, Sugarcane, Groundnut, Rapeseed and Mustard and Total Oil-seeds.

Our basic objective is to examine whether there is any indication of acceleration or retardation of the growth of our agriculture. So we have attempted not only to measure growth rates of various crops but also to indicate the direction of such rates. By growth rate in the context of agriculture we, basically, mean the trend growth rates whose value depends, over time, on the physical quantity of the relevant variable. Such a rate can be found by fitting the exponential trend. If such trend emerges to be the best fitting, we shall not only get the annual trend growth rate but also conclude that the rate of growth of the associated variable remains, more or less, constant, that is, there is constant rate of growth (CRG). In our analysis the annual average growth rates [(b-1) x 100%] of different variables have been found by fitting such a trend.

Moreover, for knowing the direction of trend (decreasing or increasing) of our agriculture, curves (1) and (3) have been fitted. If the best fitting curve be either (1) or (3) with both b and c having values less than one, there will be decreasing rates of growth (DRG), supporting the retardation hypothesis and if (3) with both b and c having values greater than one emerges to be the best fitting curve, there will be increasing rates of growth (IRG), supporting the acceleration hypothesis.

Our trend analysis has covered a long period of thirty six years from 1950-51 to 1985-86 which has, further, been subdivided into two shorter periods: (i) from 1950-51 to 1964-65, pre-Green Revolution period and (ii) from 1965-66 to 1985-86, post-Green Revolution period. In this connection, we may say that there is no unanimity with regard to the beginning period of Green Revolution. Some suggest to take it from 1967-68 (eliminating the two drought years 1965-66 and 1966-67[b] while others suggest to take it from the mid-1960's[c] . For making our analysis as current as possible we have also presented the annual growth rates of the three variables (P, Y and A) of the sixteen crops over the forty-three year period from 1950-51 to 1992-93 .

Table 5.1

Estimates of Trend Equations and D Values for Different Groups of Crops in India from 1950-51 to 1985-86

Curves		*All Crops*			*Food Crops*			*Non-food Crops*		
	Variables	*Linear*	*Semi-log*	*Gompertz*	*Linear*	*Semi-log*	*Gompertz*	*Linear*	*Semi-log*	*Gompertz*
Area	a	85.51	85.68	113.0269	68.27	86.38	110.5138	82.31	82.60	117.9787
	b	0.71	1.0075	0.7142	0.63	1.0067	0.7430	0.99	1.0103	0.6268
	c	-	-	0.9486	-	-	0.9488	-	-	0.9378
	d	0.1329	0.1524	0.0736	0.1558	0.1726	0.0960	0.1341	0.1662	0.0731
Yield	a	73.50	76.49	71.2061	70.01	73.77	70.5205	81.56	83.11	76.2388
	b	1.64	1.0158	1.1416	1.84	1.0177	1.1284	1.20	1.0116	1.1311
	c	-	-	1.0470	-	-	1.0518	-	-	1.0419
	d	0.1435	0.1168	0.0935	0.1718	0.1403	0.1104	0.1152	0.1143	0.0866
Production	a	65.01	62.02	10.4037	54.27	61.11	37.4610	57.77	63.27	17117.392
	b	2.25	1.0266	6.1404	2.73	1.0273	1.7312	2.57	1.0260	0.0036
	c	-	-	1.0116	-	1.0284	-	-	0.9951	
	d	0.0920	0.0458	0.0474	0.0865	0.0607	0.0743	0.0376	0.0323	0.0416

The entire analysis is based on official statistics published in various Government publications. Our basic data (P,Y and A) are index numbers of the three variables of the crops with the triennium ending 1969-70 = 100.

Growth of Agriculture in India: The Aggregative Study Phase 1: From 1950-51 to 1985-86

The progress of three groups of crops during this period can be visualized from Table 5.1. A scrutiny of this Table reveals that the Gompertz curve has been the best fit to yield and acreage under each of the three groups of crops while the semi-logarithmic fitting has been the supreme in case of production under each of them. Again, in fitting the acreage under each group of crops we notice that both the point growth rate determining parameters, that is, b and c have assumed values less than one while in case of productivity under the same group they have taken values greater than one. The acreage under each group of crops was thus consistent with the retardation hypothesis while productivity under the same became consistent with the acceleration hypothesis. Our trend results thus suggest that a sharp increase in the growth of agricultural production in India during the aforesaid period was not possible primarily because of the diminishing rate of growth of cropped area. Thus although the growth rate of productivity of land in agriculture is found to be rising, the growth rate of agricultural output remained more or less constant in view of the fact that the semi-logarithmic trend gave the best fit to output. These results indicate that during this period production under all crops, foodcrops and non-foodcrops, increased respectively at the uniform rates of 2.66%, 2.73% and 2.60% per annum.

(a) From 1950-51 to 1964-65

The furtherance of our agriculture in terms of those three

groups of crops during this period (on the eve of the Green Revolution) can be looked at from the trend results presented in Table 5.2 which, clearly, displays that only area under each group of crops as revealed by the best fitting trend equation (linear in case of both all crops and non-foodcrops while Gompertz curve with b < 1 and c < 1 in case of foodcrops) was subject to the diminishing growth rate, their joint effect produced declining growth rate in production, which is established by the fact that the straight line gave the best fit to production of all crops. So the trends of growth of output, yield and acreage under all crops prior to the adoption of new technology were consistent with the retardation hypothesis. The diminishing growth rate in the production of foodgrains in this period can also be explained by the similar argument. During this period output of non-food crops increased at a uniform rate (the actual rate being 3.57% per annum). But for the diminishing rate of growth of area under these crops, production under them could have increased at a still higher rate. During this period the Gompertz fitting was very poor in case of all variables except area under foodcrops.

(b) From 1965-66 to 1985-86

Coming now to the post-Green Revolution period we find from Table 5.3 that productivity under each group of crops was fitted best by the semi-logarithmic growth curve. It is also seen from this Table that yield under both foodcrops and non-foodcrops during this period increased at a constant annual rate respectively of 2.58% and 1.64% while that under all crops increased at the rate of 2.27% per annum. Area under each group of crops was, during this period like the previous one, under the operation of diminishing growth rate in view of the fact that the linear trend with the positive slope in case of non-foodgrains and the Gompertz trend with both b and c assuming values less than one in case of both foodcrops and all crops gave the best fitting trend results.

Table 5.2

Estimates of Trend Equations and D Values for Different Groups of Crops in India from 1950-51 to 1964-65

Curves		*All Crops*			*Food Crops*			*Non-food Crops*		
	Variables	*Linear*	*Semi-log*	*Gompertz*	*Linear*	*Semi-log*	*Gompertz*	*Linear*	*Semi-log*	*Gompertz*
Area	a	80.91	81.05	103.0481	82.12	82.18	99.5117	75.37	75.89	121.5322
	b	1.39	1.0157	0.7359	1.24	1.0141	0.7646	1.99	1.0227	0.5825
	c	-	-	0.8837	-	-	0.8515	-	-	0.9282
	d	0.0754	0.0887	0.0942	0.1333	0.1501	0.1255	0.0464	0.5030	0.1160
Yield	a	78.52	78.67	74.9209	76.41	76.50	70.7229	84.21	84.35	80.3117
	b	1.23	1.0143	1.0671	1.28	1.0154	1.0975	1.03	1.0114	1.0626
	c	-	-	1.0976	-	-	1.0822	-	-	1.0888
	d	0.2810	0.2815	0.3584	0.3287	0.3361	0.3959	0.3139	0.3110	0.3536
Production	a	59.65	60.48	440.2637	60.25	60.79	278.7577	58.54	59.51	579.4615
	b	2.42	1.0327	0.1319	2.27	1.0312	0.2099	2.71	1.0357	0.0979
	c	-	-	0.9822	-	-	0.9775	-	-	0.9825
	d	0.0735	0.0840	0.1292	0.1376	0.1533	0.1927	0.0647	0.0585	0.1113

During this period in the case of production figures of both all crops and non-food crops the semi-logarithmic curve gave the best fit, while for those of foodcrops the straight line gave the same result. Thus whereas production of both all crops and non-food crops was subject to the constant rate of growth, that of foodcrops was subject to the diminishing rate of growth. Production of all crops and non-foodcrops, in this period, increased at a constant annual rate of 3.04% and 2.67% respectively.

Findings of the Aggregative Study

The major findings that emerge from our trend analysis summarised in Table 5.4 on three groups of crops during the aforesaid periods can be summed up as follows:

1. Throughout the entire period of 36 years production of each group of crops was under the hypothesis of constant rate of growth and output under them increased at the uniform rates mentioned by these results in both the periods. However, in the pre-Green Revolution period it achieved a higher rate of growth while in the post-Green Revolution period it failed to maintain that rate and attained a relatively lower rate. In both periods production of foodcrops was consistent with the retardation hypothesis indicating that the new technology failed to put a favourable impact upon this group of crops. The retardation hypothesis persistent in the production of all crops in the pre-Green Revolution period changed to the hypothesis of CRG in the post-Green Revolution period and that shows that the new technology had some positive effect upon production of all crops in India in the second period.

2. The retardation hypothesis consistent with area under each group of crops persisted in the entire period and in the two subsequent periods, too. This indicates that

in the sphere of acreage the new technology failed to usher in any change.

3. Productivity under each group of crops was consistent with the hypothesis of increasing growth rate in the entire period. In the first period this was under the operation of decreasing rate of growth in case of all crops and foodcrops while in case of non-foodcrops it was under CRG. However, in the second period productivity under each group of crops came to be operated by the hypothesis of CRG.

Findings of the Disaggregative Study

Some of the major findings of this study have been summed up as follows:

(i) During the long period of 36 years each and every element of three major crops, namely rice (except its area), wheat and potato progressed under the hypothesis of CRG. Area under rice was, however, under the retardation hypothesis.

(ii) Gram and total pulses failed to show any trend during this period of 36 years. Almost similar statement can be made about jawar, bajra, maize and jute.

(iii) Almost each and every element associated with crops like sugarcane, groundnut, rapeseed and mustard and total oil-seeds exhibited DRG during this period of 36 years.

(iv) Production, area and yield under rice after Green Revolution just shifted their trend respectively from DRG to CRG, CRG to DRG and DRG to CRG. Output and area under wheat both before and after Green Revolution met the criterion of DRG with the exception that the area under it shifted its trend from the straight line in the pre-Green Revolution period to the Gompertz in the post-Green Revolution period. Potato in both output and area had the same

Table 5.3
Estimates of Trend Equations and D Values for Different Groups of Crops in India from 1965-66 to 1985-86

Curves		*All Crops*			*Food Crops*			*Non-food Crops*		
	Variables	*Linear*	*Semi-log*	*Gompertz*	*Linear*	*Semi-log*	*Gompertz*	*Linear*	*Semi-log*	*Gompertz*
Area	a	98.08	98.09	108.1913	97.42	97.42	106.9249	100.47	100.51	111.9358
	b	0.51	1.0053	0.8834	0.46	1.0045	0.8944	0.64	1.0061	0.8506
	c	-	-	0.8987	-		0.9142	-	-	0.8649
	d	0.3050	0.3109	0.2490	0.3929	0.3990	0.3194	0.3525	0.3611	0.3747
Yield	a	87.57	89.31	48.6808	84.95	87.29	55.3114	92.52	93.33	3441.5188
	b	2.54	1.0227	1.8747	2.93	1.0253	1.6324	1.79	1.0164	0.0269
	c	-	-	1.0247	-	-	1.0327	-	-	0.9956
	d	0.1382	0.1274	0.1627	0.1696	0.1542	0.1958	0.0930	0.0925	0.1221
Production	a	100.26	87.44	710.8260	81.96	84.79	31.2961	89.24	91.53	559.2202
	b	2.30	1.0304	0.1204	3.86	1.0336	2.7650	3.14	1.0267	0.1588
	c	-	-	0.9848	-	-	1.0236	-	-	0.9839
	d	0.2130	0.0915	0.1235	0.096	0.1059	0.1489	0.0639	0.0637	0.0931

pattern of trend, namely the exponential one, in both the periods.

(v) Only production and area under maize showed some specific pattern of trend in the pre-Green Revolution period. But yield of maize and all three elements of both jawar and bajra in both pre-Green Revolution and post-Green Revolution periods failed to express any type of trend.

(vi) Yield of both wheat and potato in the pre-Green Revolution period did not show any trend; they, however, did the same type of trend (DRG) in the post-Green Revolution period.

(vii) Each of three elements associated with both gram and total pulses failed to reveal any kind of trend in both before and after Green Revolution. The golden fibre crop, jute, also fell in this category. The area under total pulses was, however, the singular exception in the pre-Green Revolution period.

(viii) Production of sugarcane shifted its trend from CRG before Green Revolution to DRG after Green Revolution. However, area under it, though revealed the trend of CRG before Green Revolution, failed to show any trend after Green Revolution. Again, productivity of sugarcane showed the trend of DRG after it.

(ix) Production and area under groundnut in the pre-Green Revolution period met the criterion of DRG but in the post-Green Revolution period they failed to show any kind of trend. Rapeseed and mustard showed the same pattern of trend (DRG) both before and after Green Revolution. Production of total oil-seeds maintained the same pattern of trend (DRG) both before and after Green Revolution. But area under it, though showed the trend of CRG before Green Revolution, failed to show any kind of trend after Green Revolution. Again, productivity of oil-seeds though did not show any kind of trend before Green Revolution, showed the trend of DRG after it.

The summary of the crop specific trend results emerging from the above findings has been given in the following form so as to draw a definite conclusion with regard to whether there has been an increasing rate of growth or there has been any break in the trends of any of the variables for any of the crops under our study after the introduction of HYV technology in India in the mid-sixties.

Table 5.4
Results of the Best Fitted Trend Curves

Variables	*Periods*	*1950-51 to 1985-86*	*1950-51 to 1964-65*	*1965-66 to to 1985-86*
All Crops	Production	Semi - log (CRG).	Straight line (DRG)	Semi -log (CRG)
	Area	Gompertz with b<,1, c<1 (DRG)	Straight line (DRG)	Gompertz with b<l, c<1 (DRG)
	Yield	Gompertz with b<l, c>1 (IRG)	Straight line (DRG)	Semi-log (CRG)
Food	Production	Semi - log (CRG)	Straight line (DRG)	Straight line (DRG)
	Area	Gompertz with b<l, c< 1 (DRG)	Gompertz with b<1, c<l (DRG)	Gompertz with b<1, c<l (DRG)
	Yield	Gompertz with b> 1, c> 1 (IRG)	Straight line (DRG)	Semi-log (CRG)
Non-food Crops	Production	Semi - log (CRG)	Semi - log (CRG)	Semi-log (CRG)
	Area	Gompertz with b<l, c<l (DRG)	Straight line (DRG)	Straight line (DRG)
	Yield	Gompertz with b>1, c>1 (lRG)	Semi - log (CRG)	Semi-log (CRG)

Abbreviations: CRG = Constant Rate of Growth, DRG = Diminishing Rate of Growth and IRG = Increasing Rate of Growth.

Table 5.5
Crop Specific Trend Results

	Crops with Elements	*Before HYV*	*After HYV*
1.	Rice (O, Y, A)	DRG, DRG, CRG	CRG, CRG, DRG
2.	Wheat (O, A, Y)	DRG, DRG, Nil	DRG, DRG, DRG
3.	Jawar (All)	Nil	Nil
4.	Bajra (All)	Nil	Nil
5.	Maize (A, O, Y)	CRG, DRG, Nil	(All) Nil
6.	Gram (All)	Nil	Nil
7.	Total Pulses (A, O, Y)	CRG, Nil, Nil	(All) Nil
8.	Groundnut (A, O, Y)	DRG, DRG, Nil	(All) Nil
9.	Rapeseed and Mustard (A, O, Y)	DRG, CRG, Nil	DRG, CRG, Nil
10.	Total Oil-seeds (A, Y, O)	CRG, Nil, DRG	Nil, DRG,DRG
11.	Jute (All)	Nil	Nil
12.	Sugarcane (A, O,Y)	CRG, CRG, CRG	Nil, DRG,DRG
13.	Potato (O,A,Y)	CRG, CRG, Nil	CRG, CRG, DRG

Here we have dealt with thirteen crops having as many as thirty nine elements. Of these elements only five (output and productivity of rice, output and area under potato and output of rapeseed and mustard) exhibited, in the post-Green Revolution period, the trend of CRG. The break in trend made by output and yield of rice had been favourable but that made by area under it had been unfavourable. Output and area under potato in the post-Green Revolution period did not make any break in trend. In the post-Green Revolution period, there had been a slight improvement in the trend exhibited by output of rapeseed and mustard.

Phase 2: Trend of Agriculture in India Between 1950-51 and 1992-93

The direction of trend discussed so far will not serve our purpose meaningfully for a vast country like India where millions of rural people remain underfed. That is why together with the direction of trend the magnitudes of the trend growth rates are also very important. The trend growth rates of each of the three variables in connection with each crop in our study from 1950-51 to 1992-93 have been presented in Table 5.6.

Table 5.6
Compound Rate of Growth of Some Crops in India from 1950-51 to 1992-93

(in percent per annum)

Crops	*Area*	*Yield*	*Production*
All Crops	0.79	1.59	2.68
Food crops	0.69	1.75	2.77
Non- Food crops	1.05	1.18	2.63
Rice	0.92	1.64	2.55
Wheat	2.76	3.26	6.08
Potato	3.95	1.98	6.02
Jowar	-0.19	1.53	1.31
Bajra	0.23	1.57	1.74
Maize	1.71	0.85	2.59
Gram	-0.07	0.53	-0.04
Total Pulses	0.35	0.21	0.41
Total Oil-seeds	0.97	1.14	2.03
Groundnut	1.29	0.65	1.93
Rapeseed & Mustard	1.68	1.62	3.29
Sugarcane	1.87	1.24	3.07
Jute	0.73	0.79	1.53

A minute study of Table 5.6 reveals that in the post-independence period the progress of our agriculture is really satisfactory. The trend growth rates of wheat and potato are praiseworthy. The trend growth rates of output of all crops, food crops and non-food crops are almost identical. However, our performance in the field of pulses and, specially, in gram is deplorable.

Trend of Production of Indian Agriculture Since 1980

It is known to all that Indian agriculture in the first half of the twentieth century had to pass through a phase of stagnation. This is established by the fact that in the first half of that century the annual compound growth rate of our agriculture was just 0.3per cent (Konar, 1997). In comparison to that our agriculture had done superb in the second half of the last century and, in fact, between 1951 and 2000, the growth rate of our agriculture was more than 3.0 per cent compounded annually. Over the last fifty years or so our agriculture had passed through a series of changes. In this context the introduction of high yielding variety (HYV) of seeds, gradually increasing use of chemical fertilizers, indiscriminate use of pesticides and insecticides, extensive expansion of irrigation facilities are some of the changes worth mentioning.

Naturally, the application of HYV seeds, chemical fertilizers, pesticides and insecticides helped in improving the productivity of agricultural crops, extension of irrigation helped in bringing more and more uncultivable land under the sphere of cultivation. Thus through the integrated effort made on different lines, production of both food-grains and non-food-grains had reached so high [as revealed by Table 5.7 (a)] during the 1980's that supply of agricultural output had even outstripped the effective demand. The transition from scarcity to surplus is a matter of tremendous significance as that enabled our country to overcome the problems of concomitant political pressures associated with food-aid during the periods of previous food crises (Radhakrishna, 2002).

Phase 3:

Table 5.7 (a)
Annual Compound Growth Rates of Area, Production and Productivity of Different Agricultural Crops in India between 1980-81 and 1989-90 (in per cent)

Components of Growth and Crops	*Area*	*Production*	*Productivity*
Rice and Wheat	0.43	3.59	3.15
Rice	0.41	3.62	3.19
Wheat	0.47	3.57	3.10
Coarse Cereals	-1.34	0.40	1.62
Pulses	-0.09	1.52	1.61
Total Foodgrains	-0.23	2.85	2.74
Non-Foodgrains	1.12	3.77	2.31
Oilseeds	1.51	5.20	2.43
Sugar Cane	1.44	2.70	1.24
Cotton	-1.25	2.80	4.10
All Crops	0.10	3.19	2.56

Source: Economic Survey, Government of India, 2001-02.

At this stage of our agriculture the principle of globalization had been accepted in our country in July 1991 with the hope that the progress of Indian agriculture would be strengthened if it is left to market and through competition there would be enough prosperity in the field of agriculture.

All of us know that agriculture is a vast discipline and naturally, it is not possible to dwell on each and every aspect of this large branch. Hence to make our enquiry as accurate as possible and to make it as updated as possible, we have concentrated only on various aspects of the major food-grains produced in India, namely (1) Rice,(2) Wheat, (3) Coarse Cereals,(4) Total Cereals,(5) Total Pulses and, obviously, Total Foodgrains. The reason behind taking these crops is quite simple. Rice and wheat are the two principal crops of our country and pulses are quite rich in protein and the poor people being unable to afford animal protein, frequently use pulses. Morcover, pulses are very much liked by the people living below the poverty line, numbering about one fourth of our population of nearly 110 crores.

Phase 4:

Table 5.7 (b)
Annual Compound Growth Rates of Area, Production and Productivity of Different Crops Produced in India Between 1990-91 and 2000-01(in percentage)

Components of Growth and Crops	*Area*	*Production*	*Productivity*
Rice and Wheat	0.84	2.27	1.42
Rice	0.63	1.79	1.16
Wheat	1.21	3.04	1.04
Coarse Cereals	-1.84	0.06	1.65
Pulses	-1.02	-0.58	0.27
Total Foodgrains	-0.20	1.66	1.34
Non-Foodgrains	0.84	1.86	0.59
Oilseeds	0.44	0.66	0.61
Sugar Cane	1.72	2.62	0.89
Cotton	2.21	0.92	-1.26
All Crops	0.08	1.73	1.02

Source: Economic Survey,. Government of India, 2001-02.

The progress of Indian agriculture in the decade of the eighty's of the last century and in the decade between 1990-91 and 2000-01 can, at ease, be compared with the annual compound growth rates of area, productivity and production under each of the crops studied here.

Phase 5:

Table 5.7 (c)
Compound Annual Growth Rate (CAG) of Production Produced in India Between 2001-02 and 2006-07(in percentage)

Crops	*CAG*
Rice	1.42
Wheat	0.25
Coarse cereals	1.36
Pulses	2.40
Total foodgrains	1.06
Oilseeds	7.15
Sugarcane	0.36
Cotton	19.34

Source: Computed from Economic Survey, Government of India 2006-07.

A minute study of Table 5.7 (a) clearly indicates that the growth rates of production of all crops barring coarse cereals were fairly satisfactory in the eighty's of the last century. This rate was, especially, mentionable of oil-seeds, non-food crops, rice, wheat and all crops. A satisfactory trend growth rate in production during this decade is more due to the trend growth rate of productivity and less due to the growth of acreage under cultivation of the respective crops.

A completely different picture as reveded through Table 5.7(b) has been brought out in the decade between 1990-91 and 2000-01 when the growth rate of production of all crops was significantly less than that attained by the respective crop in the earlier decade. During this decade the annual compound growth rate of production of only wheat and sugarcane was satisfactory. It is to be noted that the growth rate of production of sugarcane almost coincided in both the decades. Again, in this decade behind production of most of the agricultural crops the contribution of productivity, though greater than that of acreage under cultivation, became weaker than the corresponding figure found in the early decade when productivity contributed much to the enhancement of the trend growth of production.

Table 5.7 (c) divulging the CAG of only production of various crops of our country discloses the similar picture as done by Table 5.7 (b). That is, in the first six years of the new millennium the trend growth rate of rice, one of the most famous crops of India, has been only 1.42 percent, that of wheat has been almost negligible. The CAG of output of total food-grains has, merely, been one percent. The picture of sugarcane is very deplorable. However, there has been some improvement in coarse cereals and pulses. A significant achievement has come in cotton and oil-seeds also.

A fundamental reason behind this sorry state of affair of Indian agriculture is a stagnant percentage of investment in agriculture. In fact, investment in Indian agriculture as a percentage of GDP at constant prices remained 1.9 in 2000-01, 2003-04, 2004-05 and 2005-06 while it remained 2.2 in 1999-2000 and 2001-02 and 2.1 in 2002-03 (vide Economic Survey, Government of India, 2006-07).

Our discussion, clearly, indicates that in the very first decade of the Indian Economy under globalization our agriculture had lost its tempo of attaining a higher growth rate in the production of both food crops and commercial crops. This had, quite obviously, given a great blow to the Indian Economy because in this decade the rate of growth of output of all crops(1.73 per cent per annum) had been less than the rate of growth of population (1.96 per cent between 1991 and 2001, as per the Census of India, 2001). If the growth rate of output of agriculture falls short of the growth rate of population, the inevitable conclusion will be poverty and more poverty. Therefore, in the very first decade of the acceptance of globalization by our country the agricultural sector has faced a crisis. This is established by the fact that the growth rate of production of each and every food item surveyed here has come down. If there is not enough production in the field, the question of bringing that in the market and thereby to get more marketed surplus is merely a myth.

Inter-State Disparity in Growth of Foodgrains in India

Let us now bring out the inter-state disparity in growth of foodgrains in our country during the decade of liberalization. This disparity in the period of eight years between 1991-92 and 1998-99 has been portrayed in Table 5.8.

Table 5.8
Annual Compound Growth Rates of Total Food-Grains in Various States of India (in percentage) Between 1991-92 and 1998-99

States	*Growth Rates*
Andhra Pradesh	-0.11
Assam	0.69
Bihar	3.58
Gujarat	3.38
Haryana	2.87
Himachal Pradesh	-0.80
Jammu& Kashmir	0.56
Karnataka	3.59
Kerala	-5.85
Madhya Pradesh	1.35
Maharashtra	0.55
Orissa	-3.09
Punjab	1.33
Rajasthan	4.97
Tamil Nadu	-0.77
Uttar Pradesh	2.68
West Bengal	2.61
India	1.81

Source: Computed from data published in Economic Survey, 2000-01.

We see from Table 5.8 that between 1991-92 and 1998-99 the annual growth rate of production food-grains in India had been 1.81 per cent. This growth rate had been nearly 5 per cent in Rajasthan. Next to Rajasthan had been the achievements of Karnataka (3.59 per cent), Bihar (3.58 per cent) and Gujarat (3.38per cent). The performance of Haryana (2.87 per cent), Uttar Pradesh (2.68 per cent) and West Bengal (2.61 per cent) can also be well recognized. But Kerala, Orissa, Himachal Pradesh, Tamil Nadu and Andhra Pradesh have fared very badly in the production of total food-grains. The performance of States like Maharashtra, Jammu & Kashmir and Assam is also very poor.

It is, thus, very clear that the era of liberalization, instead of lessening the disparity in the growth rates of food-grains produced by the majority of States, has widened the same.

Conclusion

Our trend analysis on the aggregative study leads to the following conclusion.

The new technology put its impact on the sphere of productivity under each group of crops as is evidenced by the fact that the linear trend prevailing in the pre-Green Revolution period shifted to the semi-logarithmic trend in the post-Green Revolution period in case of all crops and foodcrops while in case of non-food crops where productivity, already subject to the semi-logarithmic trend, significantly changed to a higher value as is indicated by the fact that the slope of the trend line became much more pronounced in the post-Green Revolution period.

Our trend analysis on the disaggregative study brings the following conclusion:

The cereal, wheat, maintained the same pattern of trend (DRG) even after the introduction of HYV. This, therefore, suggests that the popular belief regarding "Wheat

Revolution" (or, a "Wheat Revolution is round the corner" and so on) in India is far from correct.

In brief, we may point out that the much-talked Green Revolution has failed to put any noticeable impact on any of the commodities we have studied here and the HYV technology does not appear to be the "engine of change" in our agriculture.

Notes

(a) (i) Rudra (1970) fitted three growth curves, namely linear, exponential and the Gompertz to Indian agriculture from 1947-48 to 1964-65.

(ii) Dey (1975) fitted the exponential and the Gompertz curves to the figures of production under all crops and those of foodgrains of the Indian economy from 1950-51 to 1973-74.

(iii) Vaidyanathan (1977) fitted log-quadratic trends to both the series of indices of agricultural production and production of foodgrains extending over the period 1950-51 to 1975-76.

(iv) Bhalla and Chadha (1982) used four mathematical forms for estimating the Engel functions.

(b) Sen, S.R. in his "Growth and Instability in Indian Agriculture" stated "the droughts 1965-67 were, however, unusually severe (Page 35).

(c) (i) Sen, S.R. stated "Around the middle sixties there was a happy convergence of several things" (p. 41).

(ii) Late Professor A. Rudra in his "Indian Agricultural Economics: Myths and Realities" had pointed out the year 1964-65 to be the year terminating just before the beginning of the green revolution.

(iii) Ruddar Datt and Sundharam in their esteemed publication "Indian Economy" (Thirty-sixth Revised

Edition, 1997) had stated the pre-Green Revolution period as 1950-65 (p. 428).

(iv) Misra and Puri in their "Indian Economy: Its Development Experience" (8th Revised Edition, 1990 p. 505) had indicated that actually the seeds of the phase of Green Revolution were sown with the implementation of the programme named Intensive Area Development Programme (IADP) which was introduced in seven districts selected from seven States in 1960.

REFERENCES

1. Bhalla, G.S. and Alagh, Y.K. (1979) : *Performance of Indian Agriculture - A District-wise Study*, Sterling Publisher Pvt. Ltd.
2. Bhalla and Chadha (1982) : "Green Revolution and the Small Peasant, A Study of Income Distribution in Punjab", *Economic and Political Weekly.*
3. Chattopadhyay, M. and Bhattacharyya, G. (1986) : 'Growth of Indian Agriculture: A Reappraisal", *Indian Journal of Agricultural Economics,* Vol .42, No.1.
4. Datt, Ruddar and Sundharam (1997) : *Indian Economy,* 36th Revised Edition, S. Chand and Company, New Delhi,
5. Dey, A.K. (1975): "Rates of Growth of Agriculture and Industry", *Economic and Political Weekly,* Vo1.X No.25 & 26, June 21 and 28.
6. Konar, D.N. (1984-86) : "Principal Components of the Growth of Crop Output in West Bengal", *Arthaniti,* Calcutta University, Vol.XXIV.
7. —(1984-86) : "Growth of Rice Production in India since 1950-51", *Artha Shastra,* Vol.7 No.2, 1988.
8. Konar, D.N. (1997): "Trend of Indian Agriculture in the Post-Independence Period", *Artha Beekshan,* Vol.6. No.2.

9. Konar, D.N. (2004). *The Scenario of Population Growth in India*, Akansha Publishing House, New Delhi.

10. Konar, D.N. and Chakrabarti, S. (2008): *Developmental Issues of North East India*, Akansha Publishing House, New Delhi.

11. Misra and Puri (1990): *Indian Economy: Its Development Experience*, 8th Revised Edition, Himalaya Publishing House.

12. Radhakrishna, R. (2002) : Agricultural Growth, Employment and Poverty: A Policy Perspective, EPW, Vol. 37, No. 3.

13. Rudra, A (1982) *: Indian Agricultural Economics—Myths and Realities,* Allied Publishers Pvt. Ltd , Delhi.

14. Sen, S.R. (1977) : *Growth and Instability* in *Indian Agriculture*, Firma K.L.M, Kolkata.

15. *Statistical Outline of India 2001-02, 2002-03, 2003-04, 2004-05 and 2005-06*. Tata Services Limited, Department of Economics and Statistics, Bombay House, Mumbai-400001.

16. The World Bank (Relevant Years): *The World Development Report*, Oxford University Press.

6

The Extent of Rural Poverty in India

[Abstract

It is a fact that poverty is deep and extensive in India. Whenever we talk about poverty in India, we generally mean poverty prevalent basically in rural India because Indian economy is primarily a rural-based one. However, poverty is also deep in urban areas and, in fact, a large proportion of urban poverty is a spill over from the villages. The concept of poverty can be thought of either in absolute or in relative sense. In many developing countries poverty has been used in the absolute sense only whereas in most developed countries this concept has been used in the relative sense. In case of India the incidence of poverty has been studied only in the absolute sense.

The attempt to measure poverty in India dates back to the last quarter of the nineteenth century. Dadabhai Naoroji, Bhudeb Mukhopadhyay and W.W. Hunter tried to measure poverty in India at the end of the nineteenth century. After a long gap in 1962 a prominent Study Group of the Government of

India recommended measuring poverty in India on the basis of per capita monthly consumption expenditure. In this respect the contributions of Dandekar and Rath, Minhas and Bardhan have been known to many.

Over time there has been some change in poverty in both rural and urban areas. However, it has not been eliminated totally. For this the Government of India has introduced some schemes. However, all such schemes have as yet to make a marked dent on the poverty situation in India.]

Introduction

Poverty is deep and extensive in India. The pervasiveness of poverty in our country is both historical and for all purposes almost incurably endemic. A community's expenditure on food items is the best ready reckoner of poverty or affluence of that community. Ernst Engel (1821-1896), a famous Statistician, discovered in 1857 a law known as the Engel Law which states that the larger the proportion of expenditure on food, the poorer a family. That there is pervasive poverty in our country can be guessed from the pattern of private final consumption expenditure which reveals that in 1980-81 we devoted about 61 percent of our consumption expenditure on food items alone. It may be noted that as per the 55th round of the NSS data (July 1999 to June 2000) the average monthly per capita expenditure as percentage of total monthly per capita expenditure on food items in rural India was 59.4.For the poor section of our country (that is, over half of our population) food constitutes about 80 percent of their total expenditure. In reality, with the existing level of per capita income we can afford little elsewhere. As a result, poverty has engulfed our economy. In 1984-85 those below the poverty line were as many as 272.7 million which constitute more than one third (36.9

percent) of our total population. Of the most of the poor, more than 80 percent are in rural areas where more than 222 million persons constituting 39.9 percent of the rural population are in poverty. So, India's poverty is rightly described as rural poverty. In comparison to rural poverty the size of the urban poverty is less. The number of the urban poor is also considerable at 50.5 million which works out to be 27.7 percent of the urban population.

The Rural Nature of Our Economy

Whenever we talk about poverty in India we generally mean poverty in rural India because our economy is basically a rural-based one. According the census of 1991, 74.28 percent of our total population lived in rural India and they contributed about 33.7 percent of the total Net Domestic Product (NDP) in 1987-88 at 1980-81 prices. In contrast, 25.72 percent of our total population live in urban areas and they contribute about 66.3 percent of the total NDP. In 1960-61 the percentage of total people living in rural areas was 82.03 and they used to contribute 56.6 percent of the NDP while about 18 percent of our total population living in urban areas used to contribute 43.4 percent of our NDP. Just look at the contrast! Within the course of thirty years from 1961 to 1991 population of rural India decreased only by about 8 percent, though in the same period the contribution coming to NDP from the rural India fell by about 23 percent. According to the latest census of 2001, 72.2 percent of our total population live in rural areas and they contribute only about 27.9 percent of the total NDP(in 2000-01 at 1993-94 prices) while 27.8 percent of our total population living in urban areas have been contributing 71.1 percent of the total NDP. Thus between 1991 and 2001 population of rural areas decreased by 2.1 percent while the contribution coming to the NDP from the rural India fell by about 7.2 percent (from 35.1 percent in 1993-94 to 27.9 percent in 2000-01 (vide Statistical Outline of India,2002-03, Tata Services Limited). Such a sorry state of affair has resulted in massive poverty in rural India. Actually, a large proportion of urban poverty is a spill over from the villages. This being the case, it is natural that the causes and cures of poverty in India can be found and at the same time be solved in the socio-economic setting of rural India.

Study of Poverty in India

The concept of poverty can be thought of either in absolute or in relative sense. In many developing countries poverty is used in the absolute sense only, while in most developed countries this concept is used in the relative sense. In our country the incidence of poverty has been studied only in the absolute sense.

There are two alternative methods of poverty: (1) The direct method and (2) the income method. The former is simply to ascertain the set of people whose consumption baskets happen to leave some basic needs unsatisfied, while the latter method requires that a minimum income should be calculated at which all the specified minimum needs are satisfied. Naturally, persons whose consumption or income falls below this norm are identified as living under poverty line. The most common measure of the overall poverty is the head count measure given by the proportion of total population identified as poor. To study poverty in India the head count measure as a crude form had been used in the last two decades of the nineteenth century. It is still the mainstay of poverty in India.

The attempt to measure poverty in India dates back to the last quarter of the nineteenth century. Dadabhai Naoroji, for example, measured poverty in India on the criterion of per capita income in 1876. Bhudeb Mukhopadhyay did the same job on the criterion of per capita expenditure in 1892. W.W.Hunter in 1880 and Lord Dufferin in 1888 tried to identify poverty on the criterion of insufficiency of food or of visible privation or of starvation. After a long gap in 1962 a prominent Study Group of the Government of India recommended per capita monthly consumption expenditure of Rs. 20/- at 1960-61 all-India prices as representing a minimum level of living. On the basis of some minimum consumption expenditure per month, generally Rs. 20/ and Rs.15/ at 1960-61 prices respectively for urban and rural India, there have been a good number of studies on the incidence of poverty in the absolute sense in our country. Among such studies mention may be made of Dandekar and Rath(1971), Minhas(1970) and Bardhan(1971). Most of these studies are based on household budget data supplied by the National Sample Survey (NSS) for different years starting from 1952-53.

Trend of Incidence of Rural Poverty in India

The percentage of rural people living in the midst of poverty in different years has been stated in Table 6.1.

Table 6.1
Rural Poverty, Rural Population and Agricultural Income in India in Various Years

Years	*Percentage of rural population in poverty*	*Rural population (in million)*	*NDP of Agriculture (Rs.crores at 1970-71 prices)*
1956-57	54.1	329.47	11953
1957-58	50.2	335.63	11321
1958-59	46.5	341.80	12604
1959-60	44.4	347.96	12364
1960-61	38.9	354.13	13143
1961-62	39.4	360.29	13234
1963-64	44.5	376.04	13204
1964-65	46.8	383.92	14429
1965-66	53.9	391.79	12279
1966-67	56.6	399.67	12084
1967-68	56.5	407.55	14043
1968-69	51.0	415.42	14121
1970- 71	47.5	431.17	16354
1971-72	41.2	439.05	16209
1972-73	43.1	445.34	15118
1973-74	46.1	451.63	16298
1977-78	39.1	476.79	19045

Source: Agricultural Change and Rural Poverty, Mellor and Desai(Ed), 1986.

It is clear from Table 6.1 that a large majority of the people in rural India are poverty-stricken. They mostly come of landless laborers, small and marginal farmers, rural artisans including fishermen, backward classes and backward tribes.

The trends in incidence of rural poverty in India in the period between 1956-57 and 1977-78 illuminate the following features:

(a) The proportion of people below the poverty line is not a stable entity and there are marked fluctuations in this proportion overtime. The percentage of rural people below the poverty line sharply declined from 54.1 in 1956-57 to 38.9 in 1960-61.This percentage increased in the following year and went to the peak level in 1966-67 (and almost the same level in 1967-68). With some fluctuations it came down to 39.1 in 1977-78.

(b) An inverse relationship between the percentage of population below poverty line and Net Domestic Product (NDP) in agriculture existed in the above period and, in fact, the simple correlation between these two variables in this period has been found to be -0.473.

Let us now portray the latest picture of the magnitude of poverty in India. This has been demonstrated in Table 6.2.

According to the latest large sample survey data on consumer expenditure made available by the National Sample Survey Organization (NSSO) from its 55th Round Survey (July 1999 to June 2000), the poverty ratio on a 30 day recall basis has been estimated at 27.1 percent in rural India, 23.6 percent in urban India and 26.1 percent for the whole country in 1999-2000. The corresponding figures in 2001-02 have respectively been 18.6 percent, 16.6 percent and 18.0 percent.

Table 6.2
Estimates of Poverty in India

Unit: Number in million and ratio in percentage

Years	*No. of poor (All-India)*	*Poverty Ratio (All-India)*	*No. of poor (Rural India)*	*Poverty Ratio (Rural India)*	*No. of poor (Urban India)*	*Poverty Ratio (Urban India)*
1973-74	321	54.9	261	56.4	60	49.0
1977-78	329	51.3	264	53.1	65	45.2
1983	323	44.5	252	45.7	71	40.8
1987-88	307	38.9	232	39.1	75	38.2
1993-94	320	36.0	244	37.3	76	32.4
1999-2000	260	26.1	193	27.1	67	23.6
2001-02	182	18.0	137.5	18.6	44.5	16.6

Source: Planning Commission, Government of India.

Taken from Economic Survey, 2001-02, Government of India, Table 10.4, page 238 (up to 1999-2000) and information for 2001-02 have been taken from Statistical Outline of India, 2002-03, Tata Services Limited, page 217.

The incidence of poverty expressed as a percentage of people living below the poverty line has, thus, witnessed a steady decline from about 55 percent in 1973-74 to 36 percent in 1993-94, to about 26 percent in 1999-2000 and finally to 18 percent in 2001-02. Though the poverty ratio declined, the number of poor remained stable at around 320 million for a fairly long period of two decades (between 1973 and 1993), due to a countervailing growth in population. The latest estimates for 1999-2000 and 2001-02 reveal a significantly reduced number of poor at about 260 million and 182 million out of a total population of 997 million and 1020 million respectively.

Changes in the State-wise Incidence of Rural Poverty

Over time there has been some diminution in the

incidence of rural poverty in India. Table 6.3 will illuminate such a phenomenon.

Table 6.3 reveals that across the major States in India there is wide disparity in the incidence of rural poverty. Before the introduction of new technology Assam, Haryana and Punjab had been the only three States to have shown an incidence of rural poverty significantly below the All-India figure. Out of fifteen States as many as nine States recorded incidence of poverty higher than the All-India figure.

Table 6.3 (a)
Change in the Incidence of Rural Poverty Across Major States in India

States	*Incidence of rural poverty over years*			
	1964-65	*1972- 73*	*1977-78*	*1983*
Andhra Pradesh	41.2	46.7	30.6	19.4
Assam	20.1	38.5	38.3	23.1
Bihar	53.0	60.3	55.4	56.4
Gujarat	51.0	43.3	31.8	15.9
Haryana	24.7	16.5	20.1	12.1
Karnataka	54.4	44.1	42.5	31.3
Kerala	61.6	55.5	41.8	27.8
Madhya Pradesh	40.7	55.3	51.8	36.7
Maharashtra	60.5	60.6	54.1	34.7
Orissa	60.9	67.4	61.6	53.6
Punjab	26.0	16.2	10.9	08.7
Rajasthan	30.0	36.4	24.3	22.4
Tamil Nadu	57.8	49.8	48.8	44.5
Uttar Pradesh	53.2	43.8	38.9	37.0
West Bengal	65.7	66.5	62.3	54.7
All India	46.4	44.8	40.4	33.2
Around States				
(a) Mean	46.72	46.73	40.88	31.89
(b) S.D.	14.66	15.06	14.75	14.91
(c) C.V.	31.38	32.23	36.08	46.76

Source: The Indian Economic Review, Vol.XXIII, No.2, July-December, 1988. The Statistical Measures have, however, been computed by the Author.

In States like West Bengal, Kerala, Orissa and Maharashtra more than 60 percent of the rural population were in the grip of poverty.

Table 6.3 (a) demonstrates that in comparison to the incidence of rural poverty in 1964-65, the early 1970's (1972-73) saw a quick decline in the incidence of rural poverty in Punjab and Haryana, the two States which got most of the benefits of the New Agrarian Technology. They were followed by Karnataka, Uttar Pradesh, Gujarat, Tamil Nadu and Kerala in terms of the order of decline in incidence of rural poverty. In rest of the States the proportion of population below the poverty line increased. Since 1972-73, however, all the States, barring Bihar, have recorded successively lower proportion of their population below the poverty line.

In spite of a decline in the percentage of rural people below the poverty line, it may be pointed out that the inter-State disparity in the incidence of poverty has been steadily increasing. This has been established by the fact that the coefficient of variation in the incidence of poverty across the major States of India has been increasing from 31.38 in 1964-65 to 32.23 in 1972-73, to 36.08 in 1977-78 and further to 46.76 in 1983. Looking at the incidence of rural poverty across the major States of India in 1983, we observe that in States like Punjab, Haryana, Gujarat and Andhra Pradesh, less than 20 percent of rural people were under poverty. However, in each of the three States of East India, namely Bihar, West Bengal and Orissa, more than 50% of the rural people remained poverty-stricken.

We may now dwell on the change in the incidence of rural poverty across the major States of India during the 90's of the last century. This can be visualized from Table 6.3 (b).

Table 6.3 (b)

Change in the Incidence of Rural Poverty Across Major States of India in 1993-94 and 1999-2000

States	*1993-94 Incidence of rural poverty*	*1993-94 Ranks in increasing order*	*1999-2000 Incidence of rural poverty*	*1999-2000 Ranks in increasing order*
Andhra Pradesh	15.92	2	11.05	4
Assam	45.01	13	40.04	13
Bihar	58.21	15	44.30	14
Gujarat	22.18	3	13.17	5
Haryana	28.02	6	8.27	2
Karnataka	29.88	7	17.38	7
Kerala	25.76	4	9.38	3
Madhya Pradesh	40.64	10	37.06	12
Maharashtra	37.93	9	23.72	9
Orissa	49.72	14	48.01	15
Punjab	11.95	1	6.35	1
Rajasthan	26.46	5	13.74	6
Tamil Nadu	32.48	8	20.55	8
Uttar Pradesh	42.28	12	31.22	10
West Bengal	40.80	11	31.85	11
All-India	37.27	—	27.09	
Around States *				
(a) Mean	33.82	—	23.74	—
(b) S.D.	135.17	—	103.13	—
(c) C.V.	399.71	—	434.41	—

Source: Planning Commission, Government of India.
Taken from Economic Survey, Government of India, 2001-02, Table 10.5, Page 239.
* Statistical Measures have, however, been calculated by the author himself.

A critical analysis of Table 6.3 (b) discloses the fact that between 1993-94 and 1999-2000 there has been a quick fall in rural poverty on all- India basis (from about 37 percent to 27 percent). Similar is the case with major States of India, though there are wide fluctuations among these States. The Table reveals that in both the years Punjab headed the States in the reduction of poverty while Haryana improved its position from sixth in 1993-94 to second in 1999-2000. However, in Haryana there was 70.5 percent reduction in rural poverty while in Kerala there was 63.59 percent reduction in it between these two years. In Rajasthan there had been 48.07 percent reduction in rural poverty while in Punjab there was 46.86 percent reduction in rural poverty. However, the Spearman's rank correlation coefficient of the incidence of rural poverty among the States concerned in 1993-94 and 1999-2000 has been found to be +0.94, indicating that with respect to the incidence of rural poverty the ranks of the major States in India between 1993-94 and 1999-2000 have remained almost undisturbed. This is specially true to the four States belonging to East India, namely Bihar, Assam, Orissa and West Bengal. Another interesting feature of the incidence of rural poverty in the 90's of the last century is that though there has been a diminution in it across the major States of India, the inter-State disparity in the incidence of rural poverty has been increasing. The relatively higher value of the coefficient of variation in the incidence of rural poverty in 1999-2000 compared to that in 1993-94 is a clear testimony to it. The policy makers should bear it in mind and do the needful, otherwise there is likely to be uncontrolled disturbances across the States of India.

Factors Contributing to Poverty in India

The computation of the indices of poverty is only the initial step to the analysis of poverty which abounds in our economy. We should, therefore, try to enquire into the factors contributing to poverty by analyzing the time series data on poverty as has been represented in Table 6.1.

The fundamental reason behind the repeated and protracted ups and downs in the level of poverty can be found in the very policy pursued by the planners since the inception of planning.

India is a pioneer in initiating economic planning among the third world developing countries. With the launching of our first five year planning on Ist April, 1951, we have completed more than five and half decades of plan exercises and that has produced tangible economic gains. It is now widely admitted that our economy is no longer as stagnant as it was before independence when in the period between 1901 and 1947 (that is, in the first half of the twentieth century) production of agriculture had grown at an annual compound rate of 0.30 percent. However, after independence, more particularly, during the plan period, our economy has, certainly, been progressing and this presents a picture of growth and achievements on various fronts. The saving and investment rates have gone high enough. Some significant additions have been made to the capital stock, including economic infrastructure and human capital. Moreover, there has been the foundation of a strong public sector. Production of foodgrains has increased to a significant extent and, in fact, in the second half of the last century production of agriculture had grown at an annual compound rate of about three percent. There have been commendable achievements in science and technology, especially in information technology. Moreover, in the production of scientific and technical man power we have attained a lot. Besides, there has been a reasonably good progress in the infrastructure like power, irrigation and communications. The economic structure has been undergoing modernization with contributions of the primary sector to NDP significantly falling from 61.3 percent in 1950-51 to about 37.0 percent in 1985-

86 and further to 27.9 percent in 2000-01, whereas those of the secondary and tertiary sectors in the NDP quickly rising respectively from 14.5 percent and 24.2 percent in 1950-51 to 22.0 percent and 50.1 percent in 2000-01.

Between 1950-51 and 1985-86 our national income, in real terms, increased at an annual compound rate of 3.6 percent while per capita income during this period increased at an annual compound rate of only 1.35 percent. Again, between 1951-52 and 1985-86 average per capita real income increased from Rs. 462 in 1951-52 to Rs. 762 in 1985-86, that is, at a simple rate of 1.85 percent per annum. However, in the agricultural sector, per capita income oscillated between Rs. 405 and Rs. 415, implying a simple growth rate of only 0.07 percent per annum. The corresponding movement in the non-agricultural sector was between Rs. 593 and Rs. 1217, yielding an annual simple increase of 3.0 per cent. Further, it is to be noted that between 1951 and 1986 the growth rate of production of food grains (2.73 percent) was higher than the growth rate of population (2.10 per cent).However, in this period the per capita availability of food grains increased from 395 grams per day to 463 grams per day, showing an annual simple growth rate of 0.48 per cent.

Again, production of cereals such as bajra, jawar and ragi(the so-called coarse cereals which the poor prefer) had been stagnant. The production index of coarse cereals(with 1969-70=100) crawled to 114.7 in 1970-71 to 115.1 in 1984-85 and it declined to 96.5 in 1985-86. Between 1950-51 and 1985-86 production of gram increased at an annual compound rate of -0.07 per cent and production of total pulses increased at an annual compound rate of only 0.30 per cent.

Again, between 1951 and 1986 consumer prices increased 7.47 times. Measured by this price increase, the emoluments of employees of public and organized sector moved marginally ahead of the rate of growth of per capita income. But the rate of increase of wages of the agricultural workers in all these years was marginal, stagnant or negative; negative in Punjab, the homeland of Green Revolution, stagnant in most other states and marginal or more than marginal in a few states.

All the facts stated above pin-point that we have given more attention to the production of "development goods" at the cost of the extremely essential goods which are within the reach of the poor. In spite of a great stride in production, half the population of our country is under-nourished or they live on inadequate food due to increasing inequality of income. The effects of the involvement of large resources for development have failed to improve the diets of the poor quantitatively or qualitatively. So, behind the incredible achievements during the planning era lies the gloomy scene of inequality, exploitation, elitism, malnutrition, social backwardness: it is a scene of scarcity in the midst of abundance. So Professor Dandekar (1986) rightly concluded: "All evidence shows that the vast majority at best remained stagnant watching the economic development in the organized sector which counts for barely 10 per cent of the population, hoping that it might some day trickle down. Here lies the explanation why, while food is available and at least half the population lives on nutritionally inadequate diet, the per capita consumption of food grains does not increase." For this pathetic state of affair the objective of planning itself is held responsible. Instead of giving top priority to agriculture and allied activities and rural development, these were accorded a low priority with the inevitable result of inviting abject poverty.

Poverty Alleviation Measures Adopted

Poverty alleviation programs which came to be accepted only with the fifth plan period are based on the conviction that the so-called "trickle-down" effect (that is, a rise in agricultural production and income levels per head will be associated with a reduction in poverty) is hardly adequate to reduce poverty and that a direct assault on poverty is, thus, called for. These are basically of two types: (a) to give private productive assets to the poor and (b) to provide short term employment through public works. The problem with regard to (a) is that the assets given to the poor are often sold or transferred to the well-off for securing short means of survival and consequently, the scheme (a) followed in various States has not been quite fruitful.

During the 1970' s a number of special programs for the rural poor had been undertaken. For example, Small farmers' Development Agency(SFDA), Marginal Farmers' and Agricultural Laborers' Agency(MFALA), Drought Prone Areas Program (DPAP), Crash Scheme for Rural Employment (CSRE), Pilot Intensive Rural Employment Project (PIREP) and Food for Work Program (FWP) had been adopted. It is sad to state that none of these programs comprehensively covered the whole country. Besides, these programs were reduced to mere subsidy-giving ones, lacking any planned approach to establish the rural poor in his attempt to attain a higher level of income. Consequently, keeping the objectives of alleviating poverty, various other schemes, viz. the Integrated Rural Development Program (IRDP), the National Rural Employment Program (NREP), the Rural Landless Employment Guarantee Program (RLEGP) and the Training of Youth for Self-Employment (TRYSEM) had been undertaken. Another scheme for increasing rural employment and reducing poverty is the Jawahar Rozgar Yojana(JRY) with which the earlier programs of NREP and RLEGP have been merged. Similar other schemes have been launched in the 1990' s and also in the new century. Some such schemes are: Swarnajayanti Shahari Rozgar Yojana (SJSRY) introduced in December 1997, Swarnajayanti Gram Swarozgar Yojana(SGSY) launched in April 1999, Pradhan

Mantri Gram Sadak Yojana (PMGSY) launched in December 2000, Sampoorna Grameen Rozgar Yojana (SGRY) launched on 25th September 2001, Valmiki Ambedkar Awas Yojana (VAMBAY) launched in December 2001, Indira Awas Yojana (IRY) and National Food for Work Program (NFFWR) launched in November 2004. However, all these programs, despite some success to their credit, have as yet to make a marked dent on the poverty situation. This is so because most of the schemes for the amelioration of poverty get distorted during the process of implementation, either these are abandoned or are soft-pedalled. Hence, many experts opine that the programs of rural development should not be put under the charge of the Panchayats. Instead, special development councils should be set up in which majority representation should be given to the small and marginal farmers, the artisans and landless laborers. Unless the structure of development councils gets revolutionized, it would not be possible to implement the policies meant for the poor. The present rapport between the bureaucrat, the landlord, capitalist and the politician can be broken only by the creation of people's development councils. It is only then that a poverty eradication program has a better chance of success.

Policies Recommended for Eradicating Poverty From India

In the following paragraphs let us recommend a few prescriptions which, if followed, may reduce poverty from our country to a significant extent.

1. There can be no denying the fact that rapid population growth, especially in the rural areas, is the key causal factor that perpetuates poverty in our country. It is also a fact that the population growth is larger among the poor than the all-India rate of growth. It is usually said that low-income families include many victims of temporary bad luck. The faster growth of population

among the poor caused partly by poverty aggravates it instead of eliminating the same. This calls for a reduction in the rapid rate of growth of population in the rural areas. For this the modern devices of birth control should reach at the doorsteps of the rural poor and they should be convinced of utilizing the same. The best means for doing this is the spread of at least primary education among men and women of all walks of life. We may recall here that at the dawn of the Meiji era in 1869, the King of Japan took the responsibility for the dissemination of the universal primary education alone and no other social welfare program. Again, with the introduction of compulsory primary education in 1870, the Great Britain assured its own ascendancy in the industrial world and paved the way for a sharp decline in the birth rate. These are the obvious lessons from History. It is really a matter of great regret that we have not learnt these lessons and applied these to our country even after more than six decades of independence.

2. Together with the reduction in the growth rate of rural population in our country we should keep a watchful eye on the entry of people from neighboring countries. The census data of 2001 reveal that in West Bengal, for example, the natural rate of growth of population between 1991 and 2001 has come to a decline but the districts facing the border have shown a huge growth rate of population and this has led to a rapid growth rate of population, especially in the rural areas. Thus immigration from other countries should be stopped with immediate effect otherwise poverty cannot be eliminated from our country. Not only that the huge pressure of population may eat into the vitality of our country and that will lead to many untoward incidents.

3. The poorer section of our society should be given some minimum amount of land and the minimum means for cultivating and harvesting. They have their own labor and energy which they can not apply productively because of dearth of land. The present debate on industrialization in many States in our country gives the hint that the Governments of these States are highly in favor of industrialization even at the huge cost of agricultural land. In this respect also a hasty decision should not be taken. China's road to industrialization has not solved the unemployment problem to the extent it was expected. In the present Indian context there will be much chaos and disturbances if the farmers are thrown of the agricultural land and industries are set up. For example, the proposed Tata's small car factory at Singur in the district of Hooghly in West Bengal will throw many farmers of their land and they will be bound to be unemployed. Besides, the mere production of cars is not enough. It is also a fact that there will be no dearth of buyers for these cars as there are many prospective buyers with huge purchasing power. But the question is that these cars will not be kept idle in the garage. These must be plied on the road so that the owners' satisfaction gets maximized. Then the natural question is that since the roads are already overcrowded with traffic, will not the plying of the new cars further overcrowd the roads and damage the same? Will not the introduction of the new cars make our speed slower rather than faster? These and similar other questions appear in mind because the width of roads is already stagnant and the roads in important towns in our country are not following the standard norms. As a consequence, a few wealthy persons will,

unhesitatingly, get some pleasure in life but that will be possible only at the cost of many unpleasant incidents. So we should look before we leap and do everything in a judicious manner.

4. The principle of the Gandhiji's idea of "village self-sufficiency" or "Gram Swaraj" should be adopted as the basis of economic development. India is still now a land of villages and as per 2001 census about 72 per cent of our population live in rural areas. Hence we should pay more attention to the development of villages and for this the technique of decentralized district plan may be adopted.

5. There should be some reservation of development in favor of the weaker section of our society. They should have a share in the additional assets and income generated through public expenditure and development program. The reservation should be not on the basis of caste but on the basis of needs and requirements.

6. A very peculiar character of some class of the rural poor is that they do not generally care for what is going to happen in near future. It is because of this nature that they fail to take the opportunity of earning more. Besides, they do not cut their coat according to their cloth and their marginal propensity to consume is almost one. They should be trained for being frugal and the benefit for being thrifty .

7. The educated rural youths should be persuaded to remain mostly within the villages and should, also, be taught how to foster development in the rural areas. It should be their duty to see if all cultivable land has, actually, been brought under cultivation and to see if

production can further be increased. They should, at the same time, take various programs for the development of their own villages. Thus they should teach their fellow brothers and sisters to be frugal in expenditure, to form the habit of saving, to be more active, to give at least primary education to the boys and girls of the villages, to teach the villagers how to make a correct accounting, to inform the villagers of the latest price chart prevailing in different markets etc. They should also see that the money lenders charging high rates of interest fail to do so and the people should bank more upon the banks than upon the money lenders. They should also teach the villagers the advantages of having a small family and simultaneously the means for attaining the same.

The educated young persons performing these duties should be provided with a minimum remuneration and for this a part of finance should come from the Government. The other part may be mobilized in the following manner.

(a) The rich persons in the villages should be convinced that they should help liberally for the improvement of their own villages.

(b) Many persons coming of villages have settled themselves in the urban areas. They occasionally go to their villages to enquire of their near and dear ones. Showing due honor they should be approached to give some help for the development of their own villages. Some of the rich persons may be requested for the development of the rural areas. In order to give some incentive to these persons, money spent for these purposes may be made tax-free.

(c) Just after the harvesting season is over, each farmer may be requested to give some amount of their produce for the furtherance of their own villages. The produce so collected should be disposed of at a time when the price of the produce starts soaring.

8. More and more emphasis should be given to agriculture. There is no denying the fact that a tardy growth or a fall in agricultural production affects the income and employment of those who are below the poverty line. A deliberate choice of technology, addressed to our own and unique problem which will not keep millions of our rural brethren idle and unemployed, should be adopted.

9. Time has come to see if rural people can be appointed for doing some job in the urban areas. Thus, for example, the waste accumulated in different parts of the urban areas may be productively utilized as manures for enhancing the fertility of soil in the rural areas. If the rural people are encouraged in this direction, many problems of the urban and rural areas may be solved. This reminds us of the famous Lewis Model captioned "Capital formation with unlimited supply of labour".

10. The ponds, tanks, lakes and river beds found here and there in the rural areas may be occasionally cleaned with the help of the rural people and these reservoirs may be productively utilized for pisciculture. Naturally, many rural youths may carry on their livelihood by making themselves engaged in this profession.

11. More and more trees and plants should be planted at

whatever place it is possible. The plantation of trees will not only make our environment serene and clean but also it will enrich our surroundings with fruits, vegetables, flowers and leaves and many a problem of the rural people will be solved.

Conclusion

The most important sector of the Indian economy today is the unorganized sector forming the bulk of the rural economy. This sector is the most undisturbed sector and neither the Central Government nor the State Government is to remain worried over this sector as this sector keeps satisfied with its own activities and fails to put any pressure on the Government. In contrast, the organized sector is the most opportune sector, this sector has been thriving year after year and remains mostly in the state of disequilibrium. The fruits of development of the Indian economy are basically enjoyed by this sector. The Government, in order to keep this sector satisfied, has been doing almost everything for this sector alone. As a consequence, in the Indian economy, there have been symptoms of structural disequilibrium. To nip this structural disequilibrium in the bud, the Government must do something productive for the unorganized sector.

It is heartening to point out that since the Eighth Plan (1992-93 to 1996-97) of our country, various steps have been suggested for the control of population and spread of primary education among the masses. Besides, much more emphasis has also been given for the improvement of agriculture and rural development. A relatively greater percentage of investment (more than 50 percent of total investment) had been earmarked for the non-government sector. It is also expected that the growth rate of population in our country will be reduced to a great extent. In fact, between 1991 and 2001 the growth rate of population has become 1.96 per cent per annum. All these are the bold steps taken for the elimination of poverty from our country.

The reality, however, speaks of the other story which will be discussed in the last two paragraphs of conclusion of chapter 8.

REFERENCES

1. Ahluwalia, M. S. (1978): "Rural Poverty and Agricultural Performance in India", *Journal of Development Studies.*
2. Bardhan, P. K. (1971): "On the Minimum Level of Living and the Rural Poor—A Further Note", *Indian Economic Review,* Vol.6.
3. Dandekar, V. M. (1986): "Agriculture, Employment and Poverty", *Economic and Political Weekly,* September, 20-27.
4. Dandekar, V. M. and Rath, N. (1971): "Poverty in India, Dimensions and Trends", *Economic and Political Weekly,* January, 2nd.
5. Datt, Ruddar and Sundharam, S. K. M. (2005): *The Indian Economy,* S. Chand and Company, New Delhi.
6. Konar, D. N. (1989): "Agricultural Growth, Poverty and Poverty Alleviation Programmes in India", *Arthashastra,* Vol. 8, No.1.
7. Konar, D. N. (2004): *The Scenario of Population Growth in India,* Akansha Publishing House, New Delhi.
8. Lewis, A.: *Capital Formation with Unlimited Supply of Labour.*
9. Mellor, J. W. and Desai, G. M. (Ed) (1986): *Agricultural Change and Rural Poverty,* Oxford University Press.
10. Minhas, B. S. (1970): "Rural Poverty, Land Distribution and Development", *Indian Economic Review,* Vol. 5.

11. Mishra, A.M. and Konar, D.N. (2008): *Growth and Development of Tourism in India with Special Reference to West Bengal,* Akansha Publishing House, New Delhi.

12. *Statistical Outline of India*, 2001-02, 2002-03 and Relevant Issues, Tata Services Limited.

13. The Economic Survey, Government of India, *2001-02, 2005-06 and Relevant Issues.*

14. *The Economic Times*, Kolkata (2007): *6th June and 6th July.*

15. Todaro, M. P. and Hariss, J. R. (1970): "Migration, Unemployment and Development: A Two-Sector Analysis", *American Economic Review*, Vol. 60, No.1.

7

Economic Reforms, Employment Generation and Regional Disparity in India

[Abstract

The basic objective of the policy of economic reforms which have been in operation in our country since July 1991 is to augment the avenues for employment and thereby to ameliorate poverty from our country. It has been expected that there will be more and more competition and it is through this competition that there will be a sharp fall in the magnitude of unemployment.

However, the picture, in reality, speaks of a different story. Our study is on the employment of the organized sector alone and we have seen that with more and more progress of economic reforms instead of generating more employment, there has been a significant cut in the employment of the organized sector. Moreover, with the progress of economic reforms regional disparity has been growing wider and wider.

Besides, during the economic reforms, where competitiveness has assumed the key parameter, administration of the States has taken the challenge of enhancing SDP. The SDP has been increasing, no doubt, but the service sector is having the largest share in it, while the share of the agricultural sector has, sharply, been diminishing. Naturally, the poor performance of the agricultural sector has been causing much concern.]

Introduction

One very crucial factor hitting our entire economy is the gradual increase in the magnitude of unemployment. In this context the Sixth Five Year plan stated: "The pace of generation of employment opportunities seems to have lagged behind the growth of labour force...The number of people unemployed and under-employed has risen significantly over the last decade".

Productive employment is the only sustainable solution to progress in any country.

Naturally, employment generation has always been one of the top priorities of our Planning Commission. But, ironically, the reality is that the number of the jobless in our country has been increasing since 1991. In some cases the "golden handshake" has been given to many. The educated persons finding little job opportunities in the country have become a liability to the society. The economic reforms with the LPG package introduced in July 1991 with much fanfare have failed to relieve the situation. In fact, the recent survey reveals that it has only aggravated the problem as it has resulted in an unfair competition between the strong and the weak and the latter being overrun by the former have been lagging far behind.

Unemployment Scenario of India

Let us now present the gloomy picture of the magnitude of unemployment in India. This has been portrayed in Table 7.1.

Table 7.1
Magnitude of Unemployment in India
Unit: Number in Million

		Years	
All India	*1983*	*1993-94*	*1999-2000*
Labour force	261.3	336.0	363.3
Work force	239.6	315.8	336.8
Number of Unemployed	21.8	20.1	26.6
Unemployment Rate: (percentage of labour force)	8.3	6.0	7.3

Source: Statistical Outline of India 2003-04, Tata Services Limited.

The Table demonstrates that in 1983, 21.8 million of our total labour force of 261.3 million had remained unemployed. In 1993-94 this figure was reduced by 1.7 million to become 20.1 million. But in 1999- 2000 this figure rose to 26.6 million. This means that in the closing year of the twentieth century 7.3 percent of our labour force had remained unemployed. The widening gap between the number of job seekers and the availability of job opportunities in India is, indeed, a matter of grave concern. This is because of the fact that the high rate of unemployment is one of the basic causes of growing unrest and social evil rampant in the far and wide of the entire economy.

Growth of Population and Labour Force in India

By employment we primarily mean giving productive jobs only to the labour force of a country. In a broader sense, however, employment means productive engagement of all factors of production. Labour force of a country is a part of the population of that country: more the population more the labour force. Hence to make any study of employment meaningful and complete, we are to make a brief study of the growth of population and labour force of our country.

Today India possesses about 2.4 percent of total global land with which she has to support about 17 percent of the world population. In 1901 our population was 238.3 million which rose to 846 million in 1991 and further to 1027.1 million in 2001. Out of this total population, 741.7 million live in rural areas and the rest, that is, 285.4 million live in urban areas. A careful study of the growth of population in India between 1891 and 2001 reveals the following four distinct phases in its growth pattern. These phases are :

(i) First phase (between 1891 and 1921): Stagnant growth rate of population.

(ii) Second phase (between 1921 and 1951): Steady growth rate of population.

(iii) Third phase (between 1951 and 1981): High growth rate of population.

(iv) Fourth phase (between 1981and 2001): High growth rate of population with distinct signs of slowing down.

In the third phase the population of India had increased at an annual compound rate of 2.15 percent while in the fourth phase our population had increased at an annual rate of 2.06 percent.

What follows from the above discussion is that the high rate of growth of population in India is a very crucial factor leading to high rate of unemployment in our country.

Increasing Expectation of Life

Besides the actual number of people, another factor that has serious impact upon the employment scenario in India is the expectation of life. It is a fact that after independence, specially since 1961, our expectation of life has been increasing at a relatively high rate. Table 7.2 will display this feature.

Table 7.2
Expectation of Life at Birth (in years) in India

Years	*Male*	*Female*
1911-20	19.4	20.9
1921-30	26.9	26.6
1931-40	32.1	31.4
1941-50	32.4	31.7
1951-60	41.9	40.6
1961-70	46.4	44.7
1971-80	50.9	50.0
1981-90	57.7	58.7
2001-06	63.9	66.9

Source: Statistical Outline of India, Tata Services Limited.

It is obvious from Table 7.2 that our life expectancy, it is quite natural, has, gradually, been increasing. This has, however, gone more in favour of the women. Evidently, with the growing figure of life expectancy the concept of old age so long prevalent in India, that is, 60+, has to be changed. This amounts to saying that a few crores of people who were so long not included in the labour force of our country, will have to be included there. This is because even if the retirement age of persons employed in various fields has not been increased, these persons retiring from immediate service will, definitely, seek employment somewhere. This indirectly affects the employment opportunity of the relatively younger persons.

Child Labour

A study of the age distribution of population in our country over the last few censuses displays that nearly 58 percent (58.2, according to 2001 census) fall in the age group

15-59, called the employable age; 6 percent (6.3, according to 2001census) have age 60+ and the remaining 36 percent (35.6, according to 2001 census) have age below 15 years. Of the last category 23 percent's age lies between 5 to 14 years –many of those, though not employable, get really employed, and are known as child labour. Thus excluding the two extreme categories of persons we may say that about 58 percent of our population are included in the labour force of the country.

Work Participation Rate and Employment Scenario in India

In reality, a part of the labour force (those belonging to involuntary unemployment and otherwise disabled persons) does not participate in any productive activity. For judging the utilization of the labour force, work participation rates (WPR) are also to be considered side by side. By WPR we mean the number of workers as a percentage of total population. This rate, in the last five censuses, has appeared in Table 7.3.

Table 7.3
The Work Participation Rate in India

Census years	*Rural*	*Urban*	*Total*
1961	45.1	33.5	43.0
1971	35.3	29.6	34.2
1981	39.5	31.4	37.6
1991	40.1	30.2	37.5
2001	42.0	32.2	39.3

Source: Census of India, Relevant Issues.

When workers are classified on the basis of rural and urban residence, the WPR's of urban population are considerably lower than those of the rural one. This is largely because more young people continue for a long period in the educational system and a large proportion of them does not get immediate employment of a type which they may accept. This is also because of the fact that the rural areas are basically unorganized and the persons there make themselves employed in whatever profession they may meet.

Besides the WPR, we should also consider the percentage distribution of working population in our country in various censuses. This has been depicted in Table 7.4.

Table 7.4
Percentage Distribution of Workers by Sector

Census years	*Primary*	*Secondary*	*Tertiary*	*Total*
1951	72.1	10.6	17.3	100.0
1961	73.4	10.6	16.0	100.0
1971	72.6	10.7	16.7	100.0
1981	69.3	13.0	17.7	100.0
1991	67.3	12.2	20.5	100.0

Source. Census of India, Relevant Issues.

It is evident from Table 7.4 that since 1951 there is very little change in the proportion of workers in the three broad sectors of our economy. However, the importance of the primary sector has been declining marginally and that of the tertiary sector has been increasing marginally.

Organized Sector and Employment Generation

It is a fact that the bulk of employment in our country is provided by the organized sector consisting of both the public sector comprising of the Central Govt., the State Govt., the Quasi-Govt. and Local Bodies and the Private Sector. But this sector itself has got some obvious limitations to provide employment to all who are actually fit for getting the same. The magnitude of employment in this sector between 1990 and 2001 has been portrayed in Table 7.5.

Table 7.5
Employment in Organized Sector in India
Unit: Number in Million

Years	*Public sector*	*Private Sector*	*Total*
1990	18.77	7.58	26.35
1991	19.06	7.68	26.74
1992	19.21	7.85	27.06
1993	19.33	7.85	27.18
1994	19.45	7.93	27.38
1995	19.47	8.06	27.53
1996	19.43	8.51	27.94
1997	19.56	8.69	28.25
1998	19.42	8.75	28.17
1999	19.42	8.70	28.12
2000	19.31	8.65	27.96
2001	19.14	8.65	27.79
2002	18.77	8.43	27.20
2003	18.58	8.42	27.00

Sources: Ministry of Labour (DGE&T), Govt. of India, Statistical Outline of India 2003-04.,Tata Services Limited and Economic Survey, Govt. of India, 2005-06.

It is seen from Table 7.5 that employment in the public sector has remained almost stagnant as only about twenty million of the labour force of our country are engaged in this sector. In the early years of the new century this figure has been far less than twenty million and it has been around nineteen million. The annual compound growth rate of employment in this sector between 1990 and 2001 has been found to be 0.16 percent. This picture is slightly better in the private sector where the number of people employed had increased from 7.6 million in 1990 to 8.6 million in 2001. But in 2003 there had also been a cut in this figure and it had been 8.4 million. The annual compound growth rate of employment in the private sector between 1990 and 2001 has been calculated to be 1.45 percent. The annual compound growth rate of employment in the organized sector as a whole between 1990 and 2001 has just been 0.54 per cent.

Economic Reforms and its Introduction

There can be no denying the fact that in the post-independence period we have, undoubtedly, attained some successes in various fields. For example, in comparison to the annual compound growth rate of agricultural output of 0.3 percent attained in the first half of the twentieth century, the rate had been around 3 percent in the second half of the last century. The literacy rate in our country has, gradually, been increasing. As already noted our expectation of life at birth has also been increasing and there has been a reduction in the infant mortality rate. However, behind this bright picture lie the dark problem of unemployment, poverty, malnourishment, the galloping gap between the "haves" and "have–nots" and the like. This is the most frustrating picture of the Indian economy, in general, and rural economy, in particular. To cope up with this dismal situation various attempts had been taken especially during the 1970's which have been discussed in chapter 6 under the caption "Poverty Alleviation Measures Adopted". The principle of economic reform is the latest device in this direction.

The principal objective of the policy of economic reforms which have been in operation in our country since July 1991 is to augment the avenues for employment and thereby to ameliorate poverty from our country. The main theme of this policy is to create an atmosphere of competition. By this policy more and more emphasis has been given to privatization, globalization and market. It has been expected that there will be more and more competition and it is through such competition that there will be a sharp fall in the magnitude of unemployment. Evidently, this is a bold step for reducing a number of maladies that have crippled our economy.

Impact of Economic Reforms on Employment Generation in India

To study the impact of economic reforms on employment generation in the organized sector in our economy we have made a twelve-year analysis between 1992 and 2003. This period has, purposely, been divided into two phases: Phase 1 and Phase2. In the first phase there are six years from 1992 to 1997 and in the second phase there are also six years between 1998 and 2003. The compound annual growth (CAG) rate of employment in the organized sector in our economy in these two phases has been presented in Table 7.6.

It is seen from Table 7.6 that in the first phase the CAG rate of employment in the public sector was 0.31 percent and that in the private sector was 2.22 percent while that in the two sectors combined was 0.88 percent. But in the second phase each sector had cut a sorry figure in that the CAG rate in each sector became negative. Therefore, with the more and more progress of economic reforms there has been a significant cut in the employment of the organized sector.

Table 7.6
Percentage Annual Compound Growth Rate of Employment in the Organized Sector in India

Sectors	*Phase 1 (1992 and 1997)*	*Phase 2(1998 and 2003)*
Public Sector	0.31	-0.94
Private Sector	2.22	- 0.81
Both Sectors Combined	0.88	- 0.90

Source: Computed from employment figures portrayed in Table 7.5.

Let us now look at the employment scenario in the

organized sector by major industries in the two phases stated earlier. This picture has been demonstrated in Tables 7.7(a) and 7.7(b).

In Table 7.7(a) the CAG rate of employment in the public sector by five major industries, namely(a)agriculture, (b)manufacturing,(c)wholesale and retail trade,(d) finance, insurance, real estate and (e) community, social & personal services in both phases has been presented. It is seen from this Table that in both the phases the CAG rate in agriculture and manufacturing became negative. However, the CAG rate in the three remaining industries in the first phase was positive. It is to be noted that the CAG rate in each of the three industries sharply declined.

In Table 7.7 (b) the CAG rate of employment in the private sector by the above-named five major industries in both phases has been presented. This Table clearly demonstrates the precarious CAG rate of employment in agriculture in the private sector in phase 1. This rate in phase 2 still became negative. However, in the remaining four industries the CAG rate of employment in the private sector remained more or less satisfactory. It is to be noted that the CAG rate of employment in the private sector in the manufacturing industry in phase2 became very poor. The CAG of employment in the private sector in the remaining three industries was quite satisfactory.

Thus it is obvious that economic reforms have not ushered in a new direction to the generation of employment in the organized sector, it has rather shrunk the situation of employment in this sector.

Table 7.7 (a)
Percentage Annual Compound Growth Rate of Employment in the Organized Public Sector in India by Major Industries in two Phases

Major Industries	*Phase l (Between 1992 and 1997)*	*Phase 2 (Between 1998 and 2003)*
(a) Agriculture, Hunting etc.	- 1.38	- 1.27
(b) Manufacturing	- 0.16	-4.91
(c) Wholesale and Retail Trade	1.43	1.17
(d) Finance, Insurance, Real Estate etc.	1.13	0.53
(e) Community, Social & Personal Services	0.83	-0.22

Source:Computed from Employment figures of the Major Industries in India Portrayed in Economic Survey, Govt. of India, 2005-06.

Table 7.7 (b)
Percentage Annual Compound Growth Rate of Employment in the Organized Private Sector in India by Major Industries in two Phases

Major Industries	*Phase l (Between 1992 and 1997)*	*Phase 2 (Between 1998 and 2003)*
(a) Agriculture, Hunting etc.	- 11.85	-0.22
(b) Manufacturing	2.95	1.95
(c) Wholesale and Retail Trade	1.49	2.05
(d) Finance, Insurance, Real Estate etc.	3.76	4.11
(e) Community, Social & Personal Services	1.68	11.35

Source: Computed from Employment figures of the Major Industries in India Portrayed in Economic Survey, Govt. of India. 2005-06.

Impact of Economic Reforms on Major States of India

Let us now dwell on the impact of economic reforms on major States of India. This analysis will be carried on under three sections: Section1, Section2 and Section3.

Section 1 : Economic Reforms and per capita income (PCY) of Major States of India

It is a fact that a good indicator of prosperity of a State lies in the enhancement of PCY at the constant prices. Table 7.8 (a) gives the view of fifteen major States of India and their per capita income at 1993-94 prices in two years, namely 1993-94 and 2003-04. These states have been allotted usual ranks from 1 to 15 on the basis of their performance in PCY in both the years and we have calculated Spearman's rank correlation co-efficient.

Table 7.8 (a)
Per Capita Income of Major States of India in 1993-94 and 2003-04 at 1993-94 prices (Rs.)

States	*PCY in 1993-94*	*PCY in 2003-04*	*Annual growth rate of per capita income*
Andhra Pradesh	7416(8)	11333(9)	4.33(4)
Assam	5715(12)	6520(12)	1.33(14)
Bihar	3037(15)	3557(15)	1.59(13)
Gujarat	9796(4)	16779(1)	5.53(2)
Haryana	11079(3)	15721(4)	3.56(7)
Karnataka	7838(7)	13141(5)	5.30(3)
Kerala	7983(6)	12109(7)	4.31(5)
Madhya Pradesh	6584(10)	8284(11)	2.32(11)
Maharashtra	12183(2)	16479(2)	3.07(9)
Orissa	4896(14)	6487(13)	2.85 (10)
Punjab	12710(1)	15800(3)	2.20(12)
Rajasthan	6182(11)	8571(10)	3.32(8)
Tamil Nadu	8955(5)	12976(6)	3.78(6)
Uttar Pradesh	5066(13)	5702(14)	1.19(15)
West Bengal	6756(9)	11612(8)	5.57(1)
All-India	7690	11799	4.37

Source: The Economic Times of India, Kolkata, 5th September,2005.
Figures within parentheses indicate ranks attained by the States.

From Table 7.8 (a) it is seen that in both the years there are only seven States, namely Punjab, Maharashtra, Haryana, Gujarat, Tamil Nadu, Kerala and Karnataka whose PCYs have exceeded the all-India figure. Obviously, the first seven ranks have been occupied by these States, though there are slight variations in the attainment of rank in 2003-04 in comparison to that attained in 1993-94. In both the years Maharashtra has retained the second position, while Punjab has lowered its position from first to third and Gujarat has improved its position from fourth to first. Haryana has lowered its position from third to fourth. Tamil Nadu also has lowered its position from fifth to sixth, while Karnataka has improved its position from seventh to fifth. Kerala has, marginally, lowered its position from sixth to seventh.

Table 7.8 (b)
Classification of States of India on the basis of their PCY at 1993-94 Prices

Nature of States	*1993-94*	*2003-04*
A. Rich(PCY=> All-India Figure) (In decreasing order)	1.Punjab, 2.Maharashtra, 3.Haryana, 4.Gujarat, 5.Tamil Nadu, 6. Kerala and 7. Karnataka.	1. Gujarat, 2. Maharashtra, 3.Punjab, 4.Haryana 5. Karnataka, 6, Tamil Nadu and 7.Kerala
B. Poor (PCY < All-India Figure) (In increasing order)	1. Bihar, 2. Orissa, 3.Uttar Pradesh, 4.Assam, 5 Rajasthan, 6.Madhya Pradesh, 7. West Bengal and 8.Andhra Pradesh.	1.Bihar,2.Uttar Pradesh, 3.0rissa, 4.Assam, 5. Madhya Pradesh, 6. Rajasthan, 7.Andhra Pradesh and 8.West Bengal

Source: Arranged from information contained in Table 7.8(a).

Table 7.8 (b) classified the fifteen major States of India in two categories: (A) Rich and (B) Poor. The States whose PCY has at least been equal to the all-India figure have been brought under the "Rich" category while those having PCY less than the all-India figure have been grouped into the "Poor" category.

A close observation at Table 7.8 (b) reveals that in both the years the same seven States (with minor changes in inter-State rank) have got the status of a rich State and at the same time the same eight States (with slight change in inter-State rank) have got the status of a poor State. It may, however, be noted that West Bengal having the eighth rank in 2003-04 emerged to be the maximum PCY generating State between 1993-94 and 2003-04.West Bengal has been followed by Gujarat, the richest State in 2003-04; Karnataka, the fifth topper State in 2003-04; Andhra Pradesh with rank nine in 2003-04 and Kerala with rank seven in 2003-04, each of which has attained the annual PCY growth rate higher than four per cent(and approximately equal to or more than the growth rate attained at the all-India level).

From Table 7.8(a) we have computed the following statistical measures shown in Table 7.8(c).

Table 7.8 (c)
Some Statistical Measures Derived from Table 7.8(a)

Statistical Measures	1993-94	2003-04
1. Arithmetic Average of PCY	Rs.7746.4	Rs.11004.7
2. Standard Deviation of PCY	Rs.30785.6	Rs.46089.8
3. Co-efficient of Variation (cv) of PCY	397.42 per cent	418.82 per cent

Rank correlation co-efficient of the States in PCY in 1993-94 and 2003-04 is 0.95.

These statistical measures will help us in inferring the relative position of the States between 1993-94 and 2003-

04. Besides, these will help us to examine if there is any inter-State disparity in the growth of PCY during the period of economic reforms.

It is very interesting to see that the rank correlation coefficient of the fifteen States in 1993-94 and 2003-04 on the basis of their performance in PCY at 1993-94 prices has been 0.95, that is, almost perfect. This inspires us to say that the pecking order of the States has remained unchanged between 1993-94 and 2003-04.

We also notice that the cv in 2003-04 has been 418.82 percent while a decade earlier it was 397.42. This amounts to saying that with the on-going progress of economic reforms the inter-State disparity in PCY among the majority of States of India has been widening.

Section 2: Economic Reforms and Percentage Share of Various Components of GDP of Major States of India

We know that the three basic components of GDP are :(a) agriculture and allied activities, (b) industry and (c) services. The Colin Clark's thesis suggests that with the passage of time the share of agriculture and allied activities in GDP will come to a decline while those of industry and services will go on increasing. This is exactly what has been being experienced by the majority of the States in India.

Table 7.9 demonstrates the percentage share of the above-mentioned three components of GDP of seventeen major States of India in 1995-96 and 2004-05. In every aspect of the GDP the States have been allotted usual ranks from 1 to 17 (the case of tied rank has also been paid due attention) in both the years and the Spearman's rank correlation co-efficient has been calculated in respect of each aspect of the GDP.

Table 7.9 (a)

Percentage Share of Different Components of GDP in Seventeen Major States of India (at 1993-94 prices)

Serial No. and States	*Agriculture and allied activities 1995-96*	*Agriculture and allied activities 2004-05*
1. Andhra Pradesh	35.2(10)	27.1 (9)
2. Assam	43.4 (4)	33.5(6)
3. Bihar	47.1 (1)	36.9 (2)
4. Haryana	36.8 (8)	24.0 (12.5)
5. Himachal Pradesh	31.6(14)	27.3 (8)
6. Jammu and Kashmir	37.9 (7)	33.7 (5)
7. Jharkhand	24.1 (16)	24.0 (12.5)
8. Kerala	32.2 (13)	16.7 (15)
9. Madhya Pradesh	39.1 (5)	30.6 (7)
10. Meghalaya	29.3 (15)	24.4 (11)
11. Orissa	45.3 (2)	36.2 (3)
12. Puniab	45.2 (3)	37.7 (1)
13. Rajasthan	34.9 (12)	26.7 (10)
14. Sikkim	35.9 (9)	22.2 (14)
15. Tamil Nadu	20.7 (17)	12.8 (16)
16. Uttar Pradesh	38.6 (6)	35.3 (4)
17. West Bengal	35.0 (11)	23.4 (14)

Source: The Economic Times of India, Kolkata, 25th December, 2006. (The figures within parenthesis indicate ranks attained by the States).

Table 7.9 (a) displays that each and every State dwelt on here has reduced its share of agriculture and allied activities in GDP at 1993-94 prices in 2004-05 in comparison to that in 1995-96 (in case of Jharkhand the fall is really very nominal) and at the same time these States have enhanced their share of services in GDP at 1993-94 prices in 2004-05 compared to that in 1995-96. It is to be noted that this enhancement has, in general, been highly significant. Coming to the picture of the share of industry in the GDP of the States we, however, get a different view—as many as twelve States out of seventeen have lowered their share of industry in GDP in 2004-05 compared to that in 1995-96. Naturally, the lower share of industry in GDP in 2004-05 by these States has been more than compensated by their increased share of services in GDP in 2004-05.

Table 7.9 (b)

Percentage Share of Different Components of GDP in Seventeen Major States of India (at 1993-94 prices)

Serial No. and States	*Industry in 1995-96*	*Industry in 2004-05*	*Service Sector in 1995-96*	*Service Sector in 2004-05*
1. Andhra Pradesh	16.6 (10)	15.4 (8)	48.2 (8)	57.5 (8)
2. Assam	12.8 (13)	16.0 (7)	43.8 (12)	50.5 (14)
3. Bihar	4.6 (16)	2.5 (17)	48.3 (7)	60.6 (7)
4. Haryana	23.8 (3)	24.5 (2)	39.4 (15)	51.5 (12)
5. Himachal Pradesh	17.2 (7)	18.7 (3)	51.2 (5)	54.0 (10)
6. Jammu & Kashmir	2.1 (17)	2.6 (16)	60.0 (2)	63.7 (5)
7. Jharkhand	40.0 (1)	35.5 (1)	35.9 (17)	40.5 (17)
8. Kerala	13.3 (12)	10.6 (14)	54.5 (4)	72.7 (1)
9. Madhya Pradesh	18.4 (4)	17.7 (5)	42.5 (13)	51.7 (11)
10. Meghalaya	7.3 (14)	10.7 (13)	63.4 (1)	64.9 (4)
11. Orissa	15.0 (11)	14.4 (11)	39.7 (14)	49.4 (15)
12. Punjab	17.0 (9)	15.3 (9.5)	37.8 (16)	47.0 (16)
13. Rajasthan	18.2 (5)	16.4 (6)	46.9 (10)	56.9 (9)
14. Sikkim	6.0 (15)	5.4 (15)	58.1 (3)	72.4 (2)
15. Tamil Nadu	28.4 (2)	18.1 (4)	50.9 (6)	69.1 (3)
16. Uttar Pradesh	17.1 (8)	13.3 (12)	44.3 (11)	51.4 (13)
17. West Bengal	17.8 (6)	15.3 (9.5)	47.2 (9)	61.3 (6)

Source: The Economic Times of India, Kolkata, 25th December,2006. (The figures within parentheses indicate ranks attained by the States).

Thus, for example, Bihar, the poorest State in India [vide Table 7.8(a)] in terms of PCY, losing its share of agriculture from 47.1 percent in 1995-96 to 36.9 percent in 2004-05, has also lost its share in industry from 4.6 percent in 1995-96 to 2.5 percent in 2004-05 but has, however, accelerated its share in the service sector from 48.3 percent to 60.6 percent in the same period. Almost similar is the picture revealed by Haryana. The phenomenal enhancement in the service sector has been noticed by Kerala and Tamil Nadu. From Tables 7.9 we may thus infer that the share of the service sector in the Gross State Domestic Product (GSDP) has, sharply, risen during 1995-96 to 2004-05, while the share of agriculture and allied activities has declined quickly. Coming to the scenario of West Bengal we notice that contrary to the general belief and the claim by many people the larger part of the rise in SDP of the State during the period has been accounted for by a sharp rise in the service sector income, not income from the agricultural sector. The share of the service sector in the State's SDP has increased from 47.2 per cent in 1995-96 to 61.3 per cent in 2004-05. This has, basically, been at the cost of agriculture whose share in SDP, during the same period, has fallen by a huge 11.6 percentage points, from 35 per cent in 1995-96 to 23.4 per cent in 2004-05. The share of industry has, of course, declined from 17.8 per cent in 1995-96 to 15.3 per cent in 2004-05.

The information contained in Tables 7.8 and 7.9, thus, inspire us to state that although the GDP in India has been growing rapidly, the poor performance of the agricultural sector has been causing much concern. May be at the national aggregates, its impact is not felt seriously as yet, but poor performance of this sector is directly affecting the growth of the States' domestic product.

From Table 7.9 (b) we have computed Spearman's rank correlation co-efficient for seventeen States in two years, namely 1995-96 and 2004-05 in respect of three basic components of the GDPof the States dealt with here. In case of percentage share of agriculture and allied activities the Spearman's rank correlation co-efficient has been calculated to be 0.86, in case of the percentage share of industry in GDP that co-efficient has been found to be 0.88 and finally, in the field of the percentage share of the service sector in the GDP this has been 0.88. Thus, each co-efficient has been highly significant and this, once again, inspires to draw the conclusion that the pecking order of the majority of the States of India has remained unaltered between 1995-96 and 2004-05.

Section 3: Economic Reforms and Share in the Aggregate State Domestic Product of Major States in India

Table 7.10
Share of the Major States of India in the Aggregate SDP at 1993-94 Prices

Serial No.	*States*	*1993-94*	*Rank in 1993-94*	*2002-03*	*Rank in 2002-03*
1	Andhra Pradesh	7.40	3.5	7.01	4
2.	Assam	1.93	15	1.44	16
3.	Bihar	2.98	12	2.95	12
4.	Jharkhand	1.92	16	1.89	14
5.	Gujarat	6.10	6	6.45	6
6.	Haryana	2.78	13	2.73	13
7.	Karnataka	5.30	7	5.47	7
8.	Kerala	3.42	11	3.17	11
9.	Madhya Pradesh	4.86	8	3.74	9
10.	Maharashtra	14.58	1	13.12	1
11.	Orissa	2.32	14	1.87	15
12.	Punjab	3.88	10	3.21	10
13.	Rajasthan	4.15	9	3.83	8
14.	Tamil Nadu	7.40	3.5	6.93	5
15.	Uttar Pradesh	10.16	2	8.21	2
16.	West Bengal	6.93	5	7.68	3

Source: The Economic Times, Kolkata, the 5th September ,2005.

The Rank correlation co-efficient in 1993-94 and 2002-03 is 0.99.

We now intend to study the impact of economic reforms on the share of the major States in the aggregate State Domestic Product. Table 7.10 presents this picture of sixteen major States of India in 1993-94 and 2002-03 both at 1993-94 prices. We closely observe from this Table that in comparison to their share in 1993-94 all States except Gujarat, Karnataka and West Bengal have a declining share in the aggregate SDP in 2002-03. Besides, the States occupying the first seven ranks in 2002-03 together account for about 55 percent of the aggregate SDP, while the remaining nine States account for about 25 percent of the aggregate SDP. Not surprisingly, the States with greater economic strength have gained at the expense of the poorer ones.

Moreover, the rank correlation coefficients of the sixteen States in 1993-94 and 2002-03 in respect of the share in the aggregate SDP has been 0.99, that is, perfect. This also leads us to draw the conclusion that the pecking order of the majority of States of India has remained unaltered between 1993-94 and 2002-03.

Summary and Conclusion

In this chapter we have made an attempt to study the impact of economic reforms on employment generation and on regional disparity in India. In the context of employment generation our study is on the employment of the organized sector alone. We have seen that with more and more progress of economic reforms instead of generating more employment, there has been a significant cut in the employment of the organized sector.

In the context of regional disparity our study has concentrated on (a) economic reforms and per capita income of major States of India, (b) economic reforms and percentage share of various components of GDP of major States of India and (c) economic reforms and share of the major States in the aggregate SDP. In each such case our conclusion is that the pecking order of the major States of India has remained unaltered between 1993-94 and 2003-04 in (a), also between 1995-96 and 2004-05 in (b) and between 1993-94 and 2002-03 in (c).

Moreover, with the progress of economic reforms regional disparity has been growing wider and wider. With reference to Table 7.8 (c) we see that in 1993-94 the richest State is Punjab while the poorest State is Bihar and the PCY of Punjab is 4.12 times that of Bihar. In 2003-04 the poorest State is still Bihar while Gujarat has become the richest State. The PCY of Gujarat has been 4.72 times that of Bihar.

Besides, the co-efficient of variation of the PCY of the fifteen major States in 2003-04 has become 406.92 percent while a decade earlier it was 383.40 percent. This amounts to saying that with the ongoing progress of economic reforms the regional disparity or the inter-State disparity among the major States of India has been widening.

There can be no denying the fact that economic reforms have shrunk the employment situation in the organized sector in our economy. Besides, during the period of economic reforms, where competitiveness has assumed the key parameter, administration of the States has taken the challenge of enhancing the SDP. The ultimate analysis of the composition of the SDP, however, reveals a different picture: the SDP has been increasing, no doubt, but the service sector is having the largest share in it, while the share of the agricultural sector has been sharply decreasing and the share of the industrial sector is also steadily diminishing. Naturally, the poor performance of the agricultural sector has been causing much concern. This is specially true in case of those States still depending largely upon agriculture for their SDP growth: for example, Assam, Bihar, Uttar Pradesh, Orissa, Haryana, Madhya Pradesh and Rajasthan. It may be mentioned that most of these States have the annual growth rate of population higher than the all-India average growth rate of population. So together with the growth rate of GDP of the country the growth rate of population of the States should be paid due attention. The Planning Commission, in its quest for higher GDP growth has, however, become insensitive to the pattern of growth that is being followed.

We may also state that whether the present trend of the rise in the service sector's share in the SDP would mean that our States are proceeding towards the stages of growth, may be debatable. However, our analysis has shown that the growing importance of the service sector will lead to widening inter-State disparities in growth rates. Again, as the growth of the service sector depends, basically, upon the infrastructure base of the State concerned and the size of the State's industrial economy, the States, having upper hand, will gain more from the prosperity of service sector compared to the poorer States. Some States, in the race for achieving more SDP, have been giving more emphasis upon industries. We may cite the case of West Bengal. But the process of industrialization demands the conversion of farmland into industrial work places. However, in the developed countries there exist strict environmental laws relating to conversion of land and location of industries. It must be borne in mind that Nature is a capital asset and she ought to be regarded as such.

While following the path towards industrialization we are ignoring the fact that destruction of Nature can cause environmental disasters. China has converted huge agricultural land into industrial work places and the country's booming economy is being matched with considerable strife, especially in the countryside. Land seized from peasants for the development of industries and infrastructure has reduced their minimum subsistence base, leaving them with what is called two-mouth lands that will not feed a family of five members. This has forced members of many households to join the country's two hundred million migrants in search of work across the country.

In fine, we should recall that "India is a land of diverse countries". Politically, this may not be accepted. However, looking at the economic levels and performance of different States, this statement may not appear to be at all outlandish. The dispersion of per capita income, literacy rates, rates of urbanization and many other social and demographic indicators are all greater among Indian States. Theoretically, we expect that through mobility of various factors of production, different regions would, over time, converge to a common level of per capita income. This amounts to saying that the greater the mobility, the greater should be the speed of convergence. In India, however, there is not an iota of sign of such convergence. Besides, Indian States have different levels of potential economic prosperity and it will not be wise to disturb this level the State is endowed with.

Suggestion

Considering the multiform nature of Indian States, their various levels of potential economic prosperity, their growth rate of population, the magnitude of unemployment, the dimension of poverty across the States, the prevalence of child labour and the experience that we gather from the Chinese road to development, we should not be in haste in formulating a policy for enhancing the GDP that will lead to environmental disasters.

REFERENCES

1. *Census of India*, Relevant Issues.
2. *Economic Review*, Government of West Bengal, Relevant Issues.
3. *Economic Survey*, Government India, 2004-05 and 2005-06.

4. Ganguli, B.N. :*Dadabhai Naoroji and the Drain Theory.*
5. *Human Development in South Asia*, 1997.
6. *Human Development Report (2002)* : Oxford University Press.
7. Konar, D.N. (1999): "Pattern of Development of the Majority of States of India", *Economic Affairs*, Vol.44, Qr 4, Dec.
8. Konar, D.N.(2004) : *The Scenario of Population Growth in India*, Akansha Publishing House, New Delhi.
9. Mazumdar, K & Paul, M (1987): " Inter-State Variations in Human Resources and Economic Development ", *Artha Shastra*, Vol.6, No.2.
10. *National Human Development Report*, 2001.
11. Naoroji, Dadabhai : *Poverty and Un-British Rule in India.*
12. *The Economic Times*, Kolkata, the 2nd August, 2001.
13. *The Economic Times*, Kolkata, the 5th September, 2005.
14. *The Economic Times*, Kolkata, the 21st December, 2006.
15. *The Economic Times*, Kolkata, the 25th December, 2006.
16. *The Statesman*, Kolkata, the 30th December, 2006.
17. Statistical Outline of India, Tata Services Limited, *Relevant Issues.*

8

Impact of Service-Led Growth on Indian Economy

[Abstract

The purpose of this topic is to show that with the passage of time, especially in the second half of the last century, the path of development (as has been revealed through the sectoral composition of the gross domestic product, GDP) that has been followed in India is quite in consistence with the pattern followed by other developing countries of Asia, namely China, Indonesia, Thailand, Philippines, Malaysia, Republic of Korea and Pakistan. This means that over time the contribution of agriculture to the GDP has, radically, been coming down, that of industry to the GDP has been slowly increasing while that of the service sector has been increasing at a quick speed. However, the occupational classification of workers in India fails to corroborate the pattern revealed by most of those countries. In India the primary sector still absorbs the bulk(around 67 per cent) of the labor force, the secondary sector provides the least employment (about 13 per cent) while the service sector provides employment not exceeding 21 per cent. It is a fact that the share of services to the GDP in each and every country mentioned above has increased. But the increase has been much larger in the case of India than most others. Consequently, the service sector has emerged as the dominant sector; industry is a poor third sector contributing only about one-fourth of the GDP. Though the service sector is the major dominant sector but a minor contributor to employment. As a consequence, poverty has not been diminishing to the extent it was expected to do, across rural areas all over India. Economic conditions of rural laborers have, instead of being strong and stout, been weak and poorer. Poor performance of the agricultural sector may, partly, be held responsible for the painful plight of the rural laborers. But there is no guarantee that the higher rate of growth of agricultural output will strengthen the economic status of the workers engaged therein.]

Introduction

The purpose of this topic is to show that with the passage of time, especially in the second half of the last century, the path of development (as has been revealed through the sectoral composition of the gross domestic product, GDP) that has been followed in India is quite in consistence with the pattern followed by other developing countries of Asia, namely China, Indonesia, Thailand, Philippines, Malaysia, Republic of Korea and Pakistan. This means that over time the contribution of agriculture to the GDP has, radically, been coming down, that of industry to the GDP has been, slowly, increasing while that of the service sector has been increasing at a quick speed. However, the occupational classification of workers in India fails to corroborate the pattern revealed by most of those countries. In India the primary sector still absorbs the bulk (around 67 per cent) of the labor force, the secondary sector providės the least employment (about 13 per cent) while the service sector provides employment not exceeding 21 per cent. It is a fact that the share of services to the GDP in each and every country mentioned above, has increased. But the increase has been much larger in the case of India than most others. Consequently, the service sector has emerged as the dominant sector; industry is a poor third sector contributing only about one-fourth of the GDP. Though the service sector is the major dominant sector but a minor contributor to employment. Without entering into the reason behind it we may, at ease, say that its consequence has been very unsatisfactory in the sense that it has given rise to massive poverty across the countryside.

Theoretical Perspectives on Structural Changes

Economic development has, historically, been associated with structural changes in the national economies. It has, in fact, most often been defined as a process combining economic growth with changing share of different sectors in the national product and labor force. The most general structural changes that have been observed over a long period of time have followed a sequence of shift from agriculture to industry and then to services. Thus, an underdeveloped economy is characterized by (a) a predominant share of agriculture, (b) with development the share of industry increases and that of agriculture declines and (c) subsequently, after reaching a reasonably high level of development, the services sector increases in importance and it becomes a major component of the economy. This pattern has not only been observed historically but also holds across the countries with various levels of development. Structural shifts and changing sectoral shares are found to hold for both the national product and the work force. Some structural economists like Kuznets have empirically demonstrated that growth is brought about by changes in sectoral composition.

Sectoral Shares (in percent) of GDP in India in the Second Half of the Last Century

Three basic components of GDP of a country are: (a) primary sector (agriculture and allied activities), (b) secondary sector or industry and (c) tertiary sector or service sector. The contribution of each of these sectors to the GDP of our country has been furnished in Table 8.1.

Table 8.1
Sectoral Share of GDP (in percentage) in India
Between 1950-51 and 2000-01

Sectors/Years	*1950-51*	*1960-61*	*1970-71*	*1980-81*	*1990-91*	*2000-01*
Agriculture and Allied	55.4	50.9	44.5	38.1	30.9	26.6
Industry	16.1	20.0	23.6	25.9	30.0	25.0
Services	28.5	29.1	31.9	36.0	39.1	48.4
Total	100.0	100.0	100.0	100.0	100.0	100.0

Source: Statistical Outline of India, 2002-03, Page14, Tata Services Limited, Department of Economics and Statistics.

The above Table illustrates that at the time of initiation of planning in India the percentage contribution of agriculture and allied activities to the GDP was about 55, that of industry being about 16 and finally, that of services being about 29. Since then there has, however, been radical change in the percentage contributions of these sectors in 2000-01, that is, within a time span of just five decades. The percentage share of agriculture had, significantly, fallen from 55.4 to 26.6, that is, a fall of more than 50 per cent; that of industry had increased from 16.1 to 25.0, an enhancement by more than 50 per cent; finally, that for services from 28.5 percentage to 48.4 percentage, an increment of about 70 per cent. This is the scenario of structural changes in the Indian economy as had been observed in the second half of the last century.

Let us now demonstrate the occupational classification of workers in the second half of the twentieth century. This has been presented in Table 8.2.

Table 8.2
Occupational Classification of Workers (in percentage) in India Between 1951 and 1991

Sectors/Years	*1951*	*1961*	*1971*	*1981*	*1991*
Primary sector	72.1	71.8	72.1	68.8	66.8
Secondary Sector	10.7	12.2	11.2	13.5	12.7
Tertiary sector	17.2	16.0	16.7	17.7	20.5
Total	100.0	100.0	100.0	100.0	100.0

Source: Complied from CMIE, Basic Statistics Relating to the Indian Economy, Vol.1, All India, August 1993.

An obvious conclusion from Table 8.2 is that the occupational structure of India clearly reflects the backwardness of the Indian economy. Between 1951 and 1991, that is, within a period of 40 years the proportion of working population engaged in the primary sector consisting of agriculture and allied activities indicated only a marginal decline from about 72 per cent in 1951 to about 67 per cent in 1991. This is really significant, since a large percentage of population dependent on the primary sector is a clear indication of the prevalence of large scale disguised unemployment in agriculture and consequently, of low per capita labor productivity and prevalence of wide-spread poverty.

A comparative study of Tables 8.1 and 8.2 is indicative of the fact that in course of just four decades between 1950-51 and 1990-91 the percentage contribution of agriculture and allied activities to our GDP had come down by more than 44 whereas that of employment in this sector had been reduced approximately by 5. During the same time interval the contribution of services to the GDP had increased by more than 37 per cent while that of employment in that sector had increased approximately by 19 per cent. In case of industry the percentage increase to GDP between 1950-51 and 1990-91 had been 86.3 while the percentage increase in the level of employment in this sector was 18.7 only.

Thus the historical view that with the gradually declining contribution of agriculture and allied activities to GDP the level of employment in this sector will, significantly, fall and with the quickly increasing contribution of the service sector to the GDP there will be more absorption of labor in this sector, have been belied by the experience of development of the Indian Economy during the second half of the twentieth century.

Development Experience of Some Countries

At this stage it will be worthwhile to portray the development experience attained by some Asian countries mentioned earlier. Table 8.3 will give a focus to this direction.

Table 8.3
Sectoral Contribution (in percentage) to GDP in
Some Asian Countries Between 1960 and 2002

Sectors Countries	*Agriculture*		*Industry*		*Services*		
	(1)	*(2)*	*(3)*	*(4)*	*(5)*	*(6)*	*(7)*
	1960	*2002*	*1960*	*2002*	*1960*	*2002*	*2002***
China	*30	15	49	51	21	34	31
Indonesia	50	18	25	45	25	38	39
Thailand	40	9	19	43	41	48	33
Philippines	26	14	28	33	46	53	47
Malaysia	36	9	18	47	46	44	50
Republic of Korea	37	4	20	41	43	55	62
Pakistan	46	23	16	23	38	54	34
India	55	24	16	25	29	51	22

*Relates to 1980

Source: Papola, T.S, Page 10-11.

**Percentage Share of Employment in Services.

A significant difference between the growth pattern of some Asian countries including India has been seen in the shift of labor force with changing sectoral structure of the economy, especially in the employment share of services. A comparative study between columns (6) and (7) of Table 8.3 reveals that the highest contribution to the GDP emerging from services has been attained by the Republic of Korea. In doing so Korea had absorbed 62 per cent of labor in that sector, a commendable achievement from the standpoint of absorption of labor. In case of Malaysia 50 per cent absorption of labor in services helped it to attain 44 percent of GDP. That is, a relatively higher percentage of employment in services resulted in a relatively lower percentage of GDP. In Philippines 47 percent employment of labor in services generated 53 percent of GDP. In Pakistan 54 percent contribution by the services to the GDP had been attained by the absorption of 34 percent employment in services. Coming to India we surprisingly take note of the fact that 51 percent contribution to the GDP emanating from services had been resulted from only 22 percent absorption of labor in the services. What a poor absorption of labor in the service sector!

Perhaps we have by now come to a stage to mention that the basic distinction between the Indian experience of development from others in this group is the difference in the growth of employment and of GDP in the service sector. In all other countries the share of employment in services has been more or less commensurate with that of GDP. In India, however, the employment share has shown much slower increase than the share of GDP. This means that growth of services in India has been much less employment-intensive than in other countries.

Basic Nature of Indian Economy

The Indian economy is basically rural in nature. According to the census of 1991, 74.28 per cent of our population lived in rural areas and they contributed about 33.7 per cent of the total Net Domestic Product (NDP) in 1987-88 at 1980-81 prices. In contrast, 25.72 per cent of our total population lived in urban areas and they contributed about 66.3 per cent of the total NDP. In 1960-61 the percentage of total people living in rural areas was 82.03 and they used to contribute 56.6 per cent of the NDP while about 18 per cent of our total population living in urban areas used to contribute 43.4 per cent of our NDP. Just think of the contrast! Within the course of thirty years from 1961 to 1991 the population of rural India decreased only by about 8 per cent, though in the same period the contribution coming to the NDP from the rural India fell by about 23 per cent. According to the census of 2001, 72.2 per cent of our total population live in rural areas and they contribute only about 27.9 per cent of the total NDP(in 2000-01 at 1993-94 prices) while 27.8 per cent of our total population living in urban areas have been contributing 71.1 per cent of the total NDP. Thus between 1991 and 2001 population of rural India decreased by 2.1 per cent while the contribution coming to the NDP from the rural areas fell by about 7.2 per cent (from 35.1 per cent in 1993-94 to 27.9 per cent in 2000-01) (vide Statistical Outline of India, 2002-03, Tata Services Limited).Such a sorry state of affair has resulted in massive poverty in rural India.

In India we have the developed rural India and the underdeveloped rural India. Punjab, Haryana, Tamil Nadu, Andhra Pradesh, Kerala and parts of Maharashtra come under the developed rural India while the rest are underdeveloped where power, infrastructure etc. are big problems. Rural India is like a pyramid. The top of the pyramid is occupied by the rich farmers and businessmen who constitute 5 per cent of the population. The next of the pyramid belongs to those with a regular income and the base of the pyramid is occupied by the vast majority of the people who are daily wage laborers.

Rural India has been caught in the so-called development trap. Low incomes of the rural households are due to the lack of economic opportunities. Most of the people of rural India are unable to pay for goods and services. As a consequence, organizations feel it costly to do business in rural India, which leads to inadequate provision of infrastructure and that, in turn, leads to lack of economic opportunities and so on. Various studies even give the idea that urban poverty is predominantly due to the fact of impoverishment of rural peasantry which forces them to move out of villages to seek some subsistence living in the cities and towns. Though there have been quite a number of schemes and programmes which have been attempted by the Central and State Governments and a few foreign agencies to address the question of rural poverty, most of them have only marginal effects. Maximum percentage of the people in the poorly connected villages live on a low productivity agriculture, cattle rearing and related casual work. Because of the inability of value addition most of the villages are always at the subsistence level. Most of the poor of the villages do always distress sale.

Since industry and services fail to absorb the level of employment commensurate with their contribution to the GDP, the increasing army of labor force is bound to fall back upon agriculture as their means for subsistence. To illustrate this we proceed to the next section.

Agriculture Still the Largest Provider of Employment in India

There can be no denying the fact that India is basically a land of agriculture as it pertinently holds a very important place in our National Economy. It is the mainstay of the vast majority of our population. Even today more than 58 per cent of our working population remains in the field of agriculture (Economic Survey, 2003-04). Still now agriculture accounts for about 22 per cent of our Gross Domestic Product

(GDP) and it still provides maximum employment to our ever increasing labor force. It has been known that even now 72 per cent of our population lives in rural areas (Census of India, 2001) spreading over six lakh of villages. A very important aspect of Indian Economy is with regard to the percentage of total workers engaged in agriculture mainly as cultivators and agricultural laborers. The necessary information in this regard taken from the latest census of India, 2001 has been presented in Table 8.4

The information contained in Table 8.4 is the testimony to the fact that the bulk of our economy falls back upon agriculture and allied services.

Table 8.4
Percentage Share of Total Workers as

Industry States	*Cultivators*	*Agricultural Labourers*	*Employees in Household Services*	*Employees in Other Industries*
Andhra Pradesh	22.67	39.64	4.50	33.19
Assam	39.14	13.51	3.43	43.92
Bihar	29.17	48.18	3.87	18.78
Gujarat	27.56	24.49	1.88	46.08
Haryana	36.34	15.22	2.47	45.96
Himachal Pradesh	65.56	3.11	1.67	29.66
Jammu & Kashmir	43.37	6.72	6.23	43.67
Karnataka	29.49	26.40	3.98	40.13
Kerala	7.19	16.07	3.55	73.19
Madhya Pradesh	42.93	28.66	3.92	24.49
Maharashtra	28.56	26.85	2.49	42.10
Orissa	29.69	35.04	4.83	30.44
Punjab	22.96	16.40	3.36	57.29
Rajasthan	53.37	10.63	2.74	31.26
Tamil Nadu	18.39	31.16	5.24	45.21
Uttar Pradesh	40.92	25.11	5.33	28.64
West Bengal	19.03	24.92	7.30	48.76
All India	58.41*		4.07	37.52

*Combines both cultivators and agricultural laborers.

Source: Necessary arrangements have been made on the data taken from Census of India, 2001.

From Table 8.4 we get the idea that at the all-India level nearly 38 percent of total workers are engaged in services and other industries while about 58 percent of them are engaged in agriculture alone. The corresponding picture across the major states of India can be discerned form the Table itself.

The contribution of agriculture to the GDP in India has, significantly, been declining while the absorption of labor in this sector has not been decreasing to the extent it should have. As a consequence, poverty has not been diminishing across rural areas all over the country. Such a picture will be brought out in the following section.

Incidence of Rural Poverty Across the Major States of India

A vivid description of the incidence of rural poverty across the major States of India has been displayed in chapter 6 [vide Table 6.3 (b)] and necessary discussion has been made there.

Conclusion

Our analysis of the sectoral composition of GDP in Indian economy reveals that there has, in recent decades, been the pre-eminence of service sector as the major contributor to growth, raising its share rather sharply in the national output. As a result, we have been able to attain an annual growth rate of GDP to the extent of more than 8 percent. But such high growth rate has not solved some vital problems the Indian economy has been suffering from.

The higher GDP growth has failed to increase wages of rural laborers. Besides, even as wages of India's industrial workers have been increasing at a record rate, agricultural laborers in the country's backyard have been fighting a grim battle for survival. The real tragedy is that the higher GDP growth, improvement in macroeconomic variables and even of higher value of rupee has put little impact on the economic conditions of rural laborers. Yojana Bhawan's high-sounding talks that the economic prosperity would percolate down the landless agricultural laborers have been belied. Economic conditions of rural laborers have, instead of being strong and stout, been weak and poorer. Poor performance of the agricultural sector may, partly, be held responsible for the sorrowful plight of the rural laborers. But there is no guarantee that the higher rate of growth of agricultural output will strengthen the economic status of the workers engaged therein. We may cite the condition of agricultural workers in West Bengal where despite remarkable growth in agricultural production earnings of the agricultural workers have not improved to the entent it was expected.

In an imperfect market like Indian agriculture where supply of labour is more than the demand for it, wage rates are bound to be low. More than 50 per cent of the male work-force in India is engaged in the agricultural sector either as agricultural laborers or in agriculture-related activities. The Government realized the gravity of the situation and to come to the rescue of the workers, fixed the minimum wage rate through legislation. But we may recall that legislation alone can not solve this serious problem (like the Child Labour Prohibition Act etc.). The workers need definite program to improve their marketability outside the agricultural sector.

REFERENCES

1. Ahluwalia, M.S. (1978): "Rural Poverty and Agricultural Performance in India", *Journal of Development Studies*.

2. Bardhan, P.K. (1971): "On the Minimum Level of Living and the Rural Poor—A Further Note", *Indian Economic Review*, Vol. 6.

3. Bhattacharya, B.B. and Mitra, Arup (1990): "Excess Growth of Tertiary Sector in Indian Economy: Issues and Implications", *Economic and Political Weekly*, November 3.

4. Census of India 1991, Series1—India Paper 3 of 1991: Provisional Population Totals—*Workers and Their Distribution.*

5. *Census of India* 2001 and Relevant Issues.

6. Chenery, Hollis B and Lance J. Taylor (1968): "Development Pattern Among Countries and Over Time", *Review of Economics and Statistics*, November.

7. Chenery, Hollis Band Moshe Syrquin (1975): *Pattern of Development, 1950-1970*, Oxford University Press.

8. Clark, Colin (1940): *The Conditions of Economic Progress*, London, Macmillan.

9. Dandekar, V.M. (1986): "Agriculture, Employment and Poverty", *Economic and Political Weekly*, September 20-27.

10. Dandekar, V.M. and Rath, N. (1971): "Poverty in India, Dimensions and Trends", *Economic and Political Weekly*, January, 2nd.

11. Datt, M. (2001): The Significance and Growth of Tertiary Sector: *Indian Economy, 1950-1997*, Northern Book Centre, New Delhi.

12. Datt, Ruddar and Sundharam, S.K.M. (2005): *The Indian Economy*, S.Chand and Company, New Delhi.

13. Fisher, A.G.B. (1939): "Production: Primary, Secondary and Tertiary", *The Economic Journal*, Vol. XV.

14. Konar, D. N. (1997):. "Trend of Indian Agriculture in the Post–Independence Period", *Artha Beekshan*, Vol.6, No.2, Dec.

15. Konar, D.N. (2004): *The Scenario of Population Growth in India*, Akansha Publishing House, New Delhi.

16. Kuznets, S. (1966): *Modem Economic Growth: Rate, Structure and Spread*, New Delhi, Oxford and IBH Publishing Company.

17. Mellor, J.W. and Desai, G.M. (Ed) (1986): *Agricultural Change and Rural Poverty*, Oxford University Press.

18. Minhas, B.S. (1970): "Rural Poverty, Land Distribution and Development", *Indian Economic Review*, Vol. 5.

19. Mitra, Ashok (1988): "Disproportionality and the Services Sector: A Note", *Social Scientist*, April.
20. Panchamukhi, V.R., Nambiar, R.G. and Mehta, R.R. (1986): "Structural Changes and Economic Growth in Developing Countries", New Delhi, *Eighth Congress of International Economic Association*, Theme 4, Dec.
21. Papola, T.S. (2004): "Structural Changes in the Indian Economy: Some Implications of the Emerging Pattern", *Artha Beekshan*, Vol. 13, No.4, March.
22. Papola, T.S. (2005): Emerging Structure of Indian Economy–Implications of Growing Inter-Sectoral Imbalances, *Presidential Address, the 88th Annual Conference of the Indian Economic Association*, December 27.
23. Radhakrishna, R. (2002): "Agricultural Growth, Employment and Poverty: A Policy Perspective", *Economic and Political Weekly*, Vol. 37, No.3.
24. *Statistical Outline of India, 2001-02, 2002-03* and Other Relevant Issues, Tata Services Limited.
25. *The Economic Survey*, Government of India, 2001-02, 2005-06 and Other Relevant Issues.
26. *The Economic Times (2007):* 6th June and 6th July, Kolkata.
27. The World Bank (Relevant Years): *The World Development Report*, Oxford, Oxford University Press.
28. Todaro, M.P. and Hariss, J.R. (1970): "Migration, Unemployment and Development: A Two-Sector Analysis", *American Economic Review*, Vol. 60, No.1.

9

Population Growth, Global Warming and Economic Development

[Abstract

It is a fact that population, especially in the Third World Countries, has been increasing at a very high rate. This rate of growth of population, especially after 1950, has imposed a strong constraint on the standard of living, happiness and even survival of mankind through the spiralling consumption of the fixed quantity of resources. A study of the history of development of human being reveals that initially man had to be satisfied with the collection of food from Nature alone. In due course there was development of agriculture. Then man through further research went on towards industrialization and with it a novel way of maintaining life was discovered. However, man, in search of reaping more profit, started exploiting Nature with a great blow and with it there came pollution in our surroundings.

With the passage of time a yawning gap was created between the rich nations and the poor nations. The poor nations, in order to maintain their livelihood, started overexploiting Nature while the rich ones, in order to accumulate more and more resources, also started formulating such policies as will help them pile up wealth for their hedonistic life-style without caring for the other world where more than 2.5 billion people live in abject poverty.

As a consequence of overexploitation of Nature, there has been climatic change leading to global warming whose impact all over the world has really been very alarming.]

Introduction

The rise of population, how it has been growing and is likely to grow in future are some of the basic facts which largely influence every sector of economic and social development of a country. Human beings are both ends and means for economic activities. When in right number they are an asset but not so and it is, in fact, a liability if the number is beyond the capacity of the economy concerned. Unrestricted population growth tends to impose a strong constraint on the standard of living, happiness and even survival of mankind through the spiralling consumption of the fixed quantity of resources. Developing countries have experienced that an annual rate of growth of population to the extent between two and three percent per annum has, in most cases, negated major benefits which might have accrued from the development process. Rapid growth of population all over the world, especially in the Third World Countries, after 1950 has posed serious problems. Non-adherence to the Malthusian warning has brought catastrophe in our civilization. A natural consequence of the high growth rate of population has been rapid urbanization and a relative negligence of the rural areas. But poverty in both the urban and the rural areas has been increasing. Finding no alternative, people have been exploiting Nature in every possible manner. The Nature, in her turn, has been taking the revenge in one form or another. Consequently, increasing degradation of environment has been brought to light and peaceful living in this beautiful earth has been at stake.

Growth of Population Across the World

According to the Holy Bible, the first man of this universe is Adam and the first woman is Eve, the wife of Adam. Thereafter population of this world has been increasing in the natural way. From various sources it has been known that population of the world was only 100 million in 3000 B.C. At 1000 A.D. this population stood at 280 million. The population of this world in different years has been presented in Table 9.1.

It appears from Table 9.1 (a) that till 1340 A.D. there had been clear fluctuations in the number of people of the whole world. Between 1340 and 1500, that is, within a time span of 160 years, population of the whole world had increased by 49 million while in the next one hundred years this increment was 71 million. In the next 50 years, that is, between 1600 and 1650, this increment was only two million. However, in the next 200 years the world population doubled (from 500 million to exactly 1000 million). It took only fifty years (from 1850 to 1900) to have another 500 million of the world population. Further, it took only 30 years (from 1900 to 1930) to have the same increment of 500 million of people. Between 1930 and 1960, that is, within 30 years there was an increase of the world population by 1000 million. Also between 1960 and 1970, that is, within just ten years the world population increased by 630 million. In the next twenty one years, that is, between 1970 and 1991, population of the whole world increased by 1750 million.

Table 9.1 (a)
The World Population Over Various Years (Million)

Years	*Population*
14	256
350	254
600	237
800	261
1000	280
1200	384
1340	378
1500	427
1600	498

Table 9.1 (b)
The World Population Over Various Years (Million)

Years	*Population*
1650	500
1850	1000
1900	1500
1930	2000
1960	3000
1970	3630
1972	3720
1975	4000
1991	5380
1997	5880
2001	6200*
2020	8500*

* Estimated
Source: Colin Clark (1977): *Population Growth and Land Use*, Macmillan; U N Democratic Year Books; Britannica World Data.

Turning to the rate of growth of population of the whole world we see that between 1900 and 1930 the annual exponential rate of growth of population was 0.96 percent (less than one percent). However, between 1930 and 1960 the annual compound rate of growth of population became

1.36 percent. Finally, between 1960 and 1991 (that is, in the same time gap of about thirty years) the annual compound rate of growth of population has been calculated to be 1.85 percent. These results demonstrate that the annual growth rate of the world population has really been appalling.

However, it is true that the growth rate of population across the world has not been of uniform nature. This growth rate is really very surprising in the Third World Countries which are, more or less, caught in the second stage of the "Theory of Demographic Transition". It is a matter of serious concern that in these countries the rate of growth of population has been around 3 percent per annum. The growth rate of population in the advanced countries which have attained the third stage of the above theory is about one percent per annum. At present China is the most populated country of the world while India with only 2.4 percent of the global land has been fostering about 17 percent of the global population. From the standpoint of birth rate alone, India has topped the list of the countries facing the population problem. The annual increment of population of India is more than the total population of the entire continent of Australia. According to the last census of 2001 our population is 1020 millions. However, from a different source it has been known that at present our population has almost touched the figure of 1100 million.

Nature in the Rescue of Human Being

A study of the history of development of human being will reveal that initially man had to be satisfied with the collection of food from Nature herself. In the early days man had, freely, gathered vegetables, fruits and seeds from the plants and trees and had eaten raw meat of wild animals. In course of time the intelligent man, the most important creation of God, learnt the art of cultivation and in this field Nature showed abundant bountiness. Then with the progress and development of agriculture man learnt the technique of industrialization. However, there is an unambiguous distinction between agriculture and industry. This distinction had been made prominent by Adam Smith (1723-1790), the father of modern Economics, in his famous book "Wealth of Nations" where he said, "... in industry and commerce the forces of nature are never brought into play whereas in agriculture they always collaborate with each other." Smith added, "No equal quantity of productive labour employed in manufacture can ever occasion so great a reproduction. In them nature does nothing; man does all; and the reproduction must always be in proportion to the strength of the agents that occasion it." (Wealth of Nations, Book II; 344).

The sum and substance of what Smith suggested is that it is agriculture which creates maximum surplus. This point may be clarified with the fact that the paddy seeds worth 5 kgs sown on a fertile land may yield output of paddy even to the extent of 5 quintals. Such huge surplus is never generated in industry. That the surplus can be created in agriculture was first made prominent by the leader of the Physiocratic School of France, Dr. Francois Quesney (1694-1774). This is what he termed "produit net" (or, net production) in his Tableau Economique.

Industrialization and the Exploitation of Nature

After the development of agriculture man through further research went on towards industrialization and with it a novel way of maintaining life was discovered. Man's comfort increased, man's time and energy were saved. But we have already seen that in industry the surplus created is relatively low. So man in search of reaping more profit started exploiting nature with a great blow. Man has, mercilessly, been cutting trees of the forest and he has been killing wild animals for getting their flesh, skins, bones and other valuables. Besides, many people with the passage of time, have changed their food habit—they have become non-vegetarians instead of vegetarians. Naturally, for man's necessity many birds and innumerable animals are being killed day after day. The effect of all these unkind activities has been very dangerous—the ecological balance has been in danger. As a consequence, the nature has been expressing her wrath through drought, flood, earthquake and similar other disasters.

Moreover, the industrialists, in order to gain more profit and at the same time to reduce cost of production, have been dumping huge wastes of the firm products in the nearby forest, river bed and sea shore. These things are being done with nominal expenditure and naturally that leads to a reduction in private cost. But that has, very much, been adding to social cost. The environment is getting polluted—there is air pollution, water pollution and the like. Man's tension is increasing, there is breathing trouble and there is ear trouble and so on. Thus people fail to lead a peaceful and tranquil life—there is no peace at the place of work nor at the place of residence. We have been maintaining a higher standard of living but only at the cost of a sound physique and a peaceful mind. We have been sacrificing the avowed principle of maintaining a "good life" as propounded by the Greek economists of the ancient period.

With the growth of industrialization there has now been a continuous spree for urbanization to which we now turn.

Growing Urbanization Across the World

Urbanization is a consequence as well as a causal factor in economic development. Obviously, the rate of urban growth is an important index of the progress of an economy. There may be a number of factors leading to an increase of urbanization. These factors are: (a) the natural growth of the urban population, (b) migration from rural to urban areas and(c) the areas previously designed as rural areas passed into the urban category by satisfying some criteria. Of all these factors migration from rural to urban areas has become very significant now-a-days all over the world, especially in the developing countries. Behind this migration also lie a number of important factors, namely social, physical, demographic, cultural and communication. It has been reported that more than 150000 people are being added to urban population in the developing countries everyday. It has also been reported that the size of cities of these countries by the year 2000 is expected to double compared to 1980. It has also been reported that from Wednesday, May 23, 2007 most of the people of this world have been living in the urban areas. So long we were under the impression that most people of the world live in rural areas. But a survey conducted by North Caroliana University and the University of Georgia reveals that at present 330,39,92,252 people have been living in the urban areas while 330,38,66,404 people have been living in the rural areas. By 2030 the world is going to sustain 810 crore of people of whom 500 crore people will live in the urban areas and the remaining 310 crore people will live in the rural areas. In many cases the economic conditions of the urban poor have become far inferior to those of their rural kith and kin. With the growth of urbanization poverty in urban areas has also been increasing. In Latin American countries, for example, the number of urban poor increased from 44 million to 115 million in 1990. Another feature of urbanization has been that urban population is getting concentrated principally on Class 1 towns with a population of one lakh and above. In 1500 all over the world there were only 24 towns having population of one lakh or more whereas in 1900 the number of such towns increased to 300 and London with a population of one million became the largest city in the world.

It has been known that by 2015 the world will have 33 mega cities with population of more than eight million and more than 500 cities with population of over one million. In India between 1951 and 1991 the rate of growth of urban population had been 3.7 per cent per annum and in the same period the rate of growth of people living in the class I cities has been 5.1 per cent per annum. It is surprising to note that of the 12 highly populated cities of the world Greater Mumbai and Greater Kolkata with a population of 12.6 million and 10.9 million respectively had occupied the sixth and the tenth places respectively in 1991. According to the World Health Organization (WHO), the ideal density of population per kilometer is 2500. But the figure for Kolkata is 32000 and that for Greater Mumbai is 13,671. These results are simply unimaginable.

Another feature of urbanization is the ever growing population in the slums and shanty towns of the developing countries. Todaro in his *Economic Development in the Third World* states, "From the favellas of Rio de Janeiro and the pueblos or jovenis of Lima to the bustees of Kolkata and the bidonvilles of Dakar, such makeshift communities have been doubling in size every 5-10 years. Today slum settlements represent over one-third of the urban population in all developing countries; in many cases they account for more than 60 percent of the urban total" (P.250).According to a Report of the United Nations in 2007 about 102 crore of people have been living in the slums and bustees.For the next twenty years this number will go on increasing every year by about 27 million (The Anandabazar Patrika, Kolkata, August 5, 2007).

Therefore, the unprecedented growth of urbanization will naturally exert stress on local environment and threaten the quality of life.

Population Pressure and Sustainable Development

A growing population needs a growing supply of food which is provided basically by the "Mother Earth". Naturally, there is always a race between rising number of people in the Third World Countries and total food supplies. This race was predicted by Thomas Robert Malthus (1766-1834) in 1798 in his *Essay on the Principle of Population.* In course of time new breakthroughs in the technology of food production, commonly known as Green Revolution enabled many Third World Countries to cope with the problem of food. But since 1970 it has been noticed that in addition to the growth of the Third World population, rising affluence in the developed countries has become a major factor in the annual increase in food demands. It is a fact that population growth remains the dominant source of expanding food demands. However, rising income levels also account for an ever increasing proportion of this demand. This may be explained with an example. Across the world people in the less developed countries consume approximately 181 kg. per person per year and almost whole of this amount is consumed directly as bread and rice to meet minimum energy requirements. But an average North American consumes over 450 kg. per year. Out of this consumption only 65 kg. is consumed directly in the form of bread and breakfast cereals while the remaining 385 kg. per capita is consumed indirectly in the form of meat, milk and eggs. This means that 385 kg. of cereal grains per capita are used to feed livestock and poultry. How alarming this situation is! Will our "Dear Mother Earth" be able to sustain this requirement for her sons and daughters? Undoubtedly, there is doubt over it.

There are four critical factors of modern agricultural production which have been putting serious resource constraints on its expansion. These are: land, water, energy and fertilizer. The world food supplies may be expanded by two ways, namely (a) increasing the total amount of land under cultivation and (b) raising the productivity on existing arable land through the more intensive use of water, energy and fertilizer. But any attempt to increase productivity of land by these two means is constrained by the following factors.

Enlarging the area under cultivation has been the traditional approach for the expansion of agricultural production. But the possibility of further expansion of farm areas is limited now-a-days by the growing competition for land use by urbanization, industrial development and transportation.

Water so long learnt by the students of Economics as a "free" good, has now become scarce and naturally has become a critical input. In many parts of the globe people have been facing the problem of drinking water.

An alternative means of intensifying agricultural production on existing land is the application of greater energy inputs through the use of mechanized farm equipment. However, the sharp increases in the world oil prices have made such efforts extremely costly.

Besides, supplies of fertilizers are now becoming more costly because of substantially higher prices for phosphate and potash and alternative uses for the petroleum into fertilizer production.

Deterioration of Environment, Nature's Wrath and UN Conferences

The pressure of population, especially in many of the Third World Countries, has enhanced the demand for food, drinking water and energy. At the same time the ever growing purchasing power of the affluent citizens of the world has intensified the demand for all these materials. The resultant of these two growing pressures has been an increasing demand for food that it can not simply be met up. The hungry man, in order to sustain the supply of food from the "Mother Earth", has been exploiting her in every possible manner only to earn her wrath, curse and displeasure. To increase the supply of food, the extension of area under cultivation has been inevitable, resulting in vanishing grazing fields on which the livestock population survive. Besides, the continuous pressure of population has led to degradation of land, erosion of soil and has deteriorated our environment considerably. That has also made land in many parts of the world subdivided and fragmented and consequently, more and more land has become marginal. As a result, lands in many parts of the world have taken the shape of the sub-Saharan Africa. Again, environmental deterioration causing resource depletion has seriously affected the poor. It is rightly said, "the poor live within a bio-mass based subsistence economy—all their fundamental needs(food, fodder, fuel, firewood, cow dung, crop wastes, fertilizers, dung manures, leaf litter, building materials, timber thatch and herbal medicines) are collected (often freely) from the immediate environment. To these may be added water, which though not a biomass itself is biomass related and crucial for survival". (The State of India's Environment, 1984-85, The Second Citizen's Report).

After the appearance of the two path-breaking titles "Silent Spring" by Rachel Carson and "Limits to Growth" by the Club of Rome, a realization dawned upon a large section of international community that "nations' farms, factories and vehicles" were turning into "seed-beds of pollution" and causing rapid deterioration of environment all over the world. To deliberate upon the issue, a high-level United Nations' Conference was held at Stockholm in 1972. Many Heads of Government attended it. Mrs. Indira Gandhi, our former Prime Minister, joined it and she made her famous observation: "Poverty is the worst pollutant" which had added a new dimension to the issue.

Immediately after the conference, the United Nations Environment Programme was founded and hundreds of conferences, seminars and symposia were held on the subject all over the world. In 1983, the Brundtland Commission was set up. In the Report captioned "Our Common Future", the Commission recommended a pattern of sustainable development. The UN Conference in Rio de Janeiro held in 1992 created a record in the massiveness of its attendance and publicity. Then came the World Summit on Social Development (1995), Habitat 11 (1996) and a host of other conferences on related items, namely water, sanitation, soil, forestry, climate change etc. However, the net results of all these conferences are almost bleak. This is because of the fact that more people are now living in absolute poverty, more are inhabiting in stinking slums; more elements of life-support systems are under stress, more eco-systems are on the decline, more species are facing extinction and more ominous looks the specter of climate change than when these conferences were held. For illustration, the water and sanitation decades were of mid 1970's and 1980's. During this decade, National Government and International agencies committed themselves to "making safe water and sanitation accessible to all by 1990". However, the tragedy is that even in 2007, that is, even after the complete end of the deadline, 2.4 billion people of the world have no facility of sanitation and 1.7 billion of clean water. Similarly, the United Nations' Conferences on Habitats, starting from the Vancouver Conference of 1976, have been passing resolution after resolution, affirming their resolve to rid the world of slums and squatters settlements. Once again, the tragedy is that these settlements have been multiplying. Now they house a population of a billion people.

Of late, a UN Report in February 2007 reveals that rain forests in Indonesia and Malaysia are being cut at such a fast rate that in another fifteen years, about 98 per cent of these would be lost, resulting in increased greenhouse gas emissions to the extent of 20 per cent. The number of environmental refugees is already nearing 50 million. Bio-diversity losses were sought to be reversed by 2010. However, recent data reveal that the wind is blowing in the opposite direction. Today about 60 per cent of the eco-systems are on the decline and two out of five species, including a quarter of all mammals, are under threat of extinction. On March 22, 2007 that is , on the last but one World Water Day, it was estimated that by 2025 about 67 percent of the world population would have to struggle hard to get adequate water. Even today, over 100 crores of people all over the world have no option but to drink polluted water the consequences of which cause death of about 3.5 per cent of them every year. The Millennium Development Goals (2000) notwithstanding, 3900 children die every day on account of water-borne diseases.

As a fall-out of industrialization and urbanization, forests and wetlands are being destroyed. Stock of fossil fuel and other minerals is getting exhausted. The level of underground water is steadily going down. The ozen layer at the stratosphere is getting depleted, making way for almost uninterrupted entry of harmful ultraviolet rays from the sun. Tropical rain-forest, once considered as the lungs of the planet, generating over 20 percent of oxygen, is being rapidly destroyed by the wood and paper-pulp traders of the West.

Following a series of events the world over, it is now almost conclusively established that global warming caused by green house gases (GHG), comprising about 77 percent of carbon dioxide, is a myth. In an article published a few years back in the British Journal, Nature, it was estimated that over one million species of plants and animals, one-fourth of all life in the world, would be extinct within 2050 due to man-made climate change.

During a recent sitting in Bangkok, the Inter-Government Panel on Climate Change (IPCC) reported that emission of GHG has gone up by 70 percent between 1970 and 2004.

Carbon dioxide has increased by 80 percent. Increase of GHG during the period was maximum in the power generation sector—about 145 per cent, next was vehicular emission—120 per cent, followed by industrial emission—65 per cent.

Through globalization, policies are being so formulated as to help the rich countries pile up wealth for lifting their hedonistic life-style without caring for the other world where more than 2.5 billion people live in abject poverty. More than 10 million children die each year before attaining the age of five. Around one billion people lack access to safe water and some 1.75 million die each year due to cholera, dysentery and other diarrheal diseases. The richest 10 per cent of the world own 85 per cent of the global assets whereas the bottom half only one per cent The inequality between the rich and the poor is on the rise in countries where about 80 per cent of the global population lives.

The information portrayed through the above-mentioned statistics has been happening at a time when top level experts and International agencies have been warning the people repeatedly about the great loss that could be caused by the climatic change.

Causes of Global Warming

The major causes of global warming are the emission of green house gases like carbon dioxide, methane, nitrous oxide etc. into the atmosphere. The major source of carbon dioxide is the power plants. These power plants emit large amount of carbon dioxide produced from burning of fossil fuels for the purpose of electricity generation. About 20 per cent of carbon dioxide emitted in the atmosphere comes from burning of gasoline in the engines of the vehicles. This is true for most of the developed countries. Buildings, both commercial and residential, represent a large source of global warming pollution than cars and trucks. Building of these structures requires a lot of fuel to be burnt which emits a large amount of carbon dioxide in the atmosphere.

Some housing appliances are also held responsible for such warming. The advent of synthetic refrigerants in place of natural ones in the domestic refrigerators in the form of CFC's (Chloro Flora Carbons) has also contributed such warming. The leakage of CFC's into the atmosphere mainly after the operation of refrigerator is over, results in the decomposition of CFC into Fluorine and Chlorine. These gases convert ozone to oxygen resulting in the depletion of the ozone layer. This ozone layer is responsible for preventing harmful ultraviolet rays into the earth, which are known to cause skin cancer.

Impact of Global Warming

Some of the disastrous impacts of global warming have already been explained. More such impacts will now be portrayed here.

Coming to the scenario of India we notice that almost all our rivers have virtually become sewers. The Great Ganges, a real lifeline of the Indian Economy, in the opinion of the World Wide Fund for Nature, has been dying. Besides, the Ganga basin has also been choking up. Moreover, the colossal Sunderbans delta not only serving as a home for the Royal Bengal Tigers but also nursing a significant part of India's rich bio-diversity—289 terrestrial, 219 aquatic, 1276 fish and 31 crustaceans' species, is also in a dangerous state. The Yamuna, another crucial river in India, has been even sicker than the Ganga. Even during the period of operation of the Yamuna Action Plan from 1993 onwards its biochemical oxygen demand-load has been increasing. What is more dangerous is that the main source of water in our country, the Himalayan glaciers have, alarmingly, been receding. Between 1971 and 2004 this recession occurred at an average rate of about 18 meters per annum. According to a Report published in the Anandabazar Patrika dt. 2.7.2007, it is due to the global warming that the great Shiva Deity formed of ice at Amaranth has been melting and naturally, the innumerable pious tourists will be deprived of a rare visit to the God Shiva. Not only that the villain global warming has been putting its paw on other religious places covered with ice, frost and fog. For illustration, the Gomukh where the melting rate of the glacier since 1970 has been double. The basic reason behind this is the high warming and emission of Green House Gas. According to many experts, the regular haunting of the tourists and many people for various reasons has put an unhealthy atmosphere on this glacier leading to a reduction in its size. If this process continues, one day will come when the Great Ganga will have to flow only with the rain-fed water. We can not simply imagine what will happen in such a situation.

Conclusion

Realizing the gravity of the situation of global warming an understanding has been arrived at the International level. In the first week of June 2007 the Conference of G-8 countries (the eight most wealthy nations of the world, namely the USA, the Great Britain, Germany, France, Japan, Canada, Russia and Italy. These eight countries together possess about 65 per cent of the global wealth.) of the world took place in Rostak in Germany and the leaders of these countries talked much about global warming, the principal theme of that year's Conference. Six of these countries, barring the USA and Russia, have promised that by 2050 they will reduce the emission of Green House Gas by at least 50 per cent.

We can help in reducing global warming by turning our air conditions down by even one degree or by turning off phone chargers and other electronic equipment when they are not being used. If each of us does our bit, we will be helping to keep global warming from harming our countries.

Suggested Polices

It is a fact that the impact of global warming is very much appalling. It is high time that we, the people all over the world, realize this and apply common sense and do the needful to make this beautiful world an abode for residing with the surroundings all around us in peace and tranquillity. To achieve this, the following strategies may be recommended at the initial stage.

1. As per the recommendation of the IPCC, the richer section of the world should cut down the use of natural resources and reduce pollution substantially.
2. Since even in the 21st century about 25 per cent of Indian people live under BPL, in our development program we should put stress on the under privileged section. We should adopt such technology as will disturb the environment and the eco-system the least.
3. Much water and electricity can be saved by avoiding wastage and by using more efficient appliances. Dependence on fossil fuel has to be reduced. We should say "no" to the nuclear power. With huge solar and wind energy available in our country, we should fully utilize them. Small hydropower is another source of clean energy which can be generated with natural falls, run of river and back water. Quite a few such installations have been working successfully. Bio fuels derived from agricultural residues and the seeds of neem, jatropha, ratanjyot and some other trees may play an important role in the transport sector.
4. It may be mentioned that about five lakh women and children die each year due to diseases related to smoke emitted during cooking. Such a precarious incident may be avoided if a bio-gas plant needing only vegetable residues, waste food, green leaves etc. can be used. It requires only 1 kg of feedstock against 40 kg of

cowdung. More than 700 such units have already been installed in Maharastra.

Besides the above, we recommend the following strategies:

(a) The rate of growth of population should be checked to the maximum possible extent. The present annual growth rate of population of around 3 per cent should be reduced to around 1 per cent. For this education should be spread at all levels and women are to be involved in every possible manner. We should give more emphasis upon the dissemination of education, not of literacy.

(b) People should be made aware of the environment. To make this effective, study of environment should be made a compulsory subject in the school education. Besides, the "World Environment Day", the 5th day of June every year, should be celebrated in such a manner that people of all walks of life, specially the children and the younger ones, realize it wholeheartedly.

(c) The environmental damaging activities should be forbidden by all means and for this strict vigilance should be kept throughout the year. At the same time environment fostering activities should be rewarded and encouraged.

(d) There should be a limit to the running of vehicles along the streets and roads of the towns. The purchase of cars and other vehicles should be on the basis of urgency of necessity, not on the basis of the ability to afford them.

(e) The relatively small towns should be endowed with new industrial centers and be provided with the basic amenities of life.

(f) The living conditions of villages should be improved. More and more emphasis should be put on the development of agriculture, rural industry and rural development.

REFERENCES

1. Bose, A. (1974): *Studies on India's Urbanization 1901-1971*, Tata McGraw Hill Publishing Company Ltd., New Delhi.
2. Colin Clark (1977): *Population Growth and Land Use*, Macmillan; UN Democratic Year Books; Britannica World Data.
3. Konar, D.N. (1991):"Degree of Urbanization in Orissa and Bihar—An Econometric Analysis", *Arthashastra*, Vol. 10, Nos. 1 and 2, Kolkata.
4. Konar, D.N. (1996): "Urbanization in West Bengal and the Problem of Environment", *Economic Affairs*, Vol. 41, Qr. 1, January-March, Kolkata.
5. Konar, D.N. (2004): *The Scenario of Population Growth in India*, Akansha Publishing House, New Delhi.
6. Konar, D.N. (1996) "Population Growth, Sustainable Development and a Threat to Environment" in *Sustainable Economic Development and Environment, India and Other Low Income Economies (Ed)* R.K.Sen and K.C.Roy, Atlantic Publishers and Distributors, New Delhi.
7. Konar, D.N.(1995): "Population Growth, Agricultural Development and the Problem of Environment in India" in *Environment and Sustainable Agricultural Development*, Vol.1 (Ed): K.C.Roy, R.K.Sen and Clement A. Tisdel, New Age International (P) Limited, Publishers.
8. Schumpeter, Joseph: *History of Economic Analysis.*
9. Smith, Adam: *Wealth of Nations*, Vol. 1 and 2.
10. *The Ananda Bazar Patrika (2007)*, Kolkata, August, 5.
11. *The Statesman* (1996), Kolkata, May 6, June 29, August 5.
12. Todaro, M. (1987): *Economic Development in the Third World*, Orient Longman, New Delhi.
13. *The World Development Report*, the Relevant Issues.
14. *The World Resources Report, 1996-97.*
15. Website http://www.globalwarming.org.in/

10

WTO and Its Impact on India's Foreign Trade with Special Reference to the Agricultural Sector

[Abstract

More than thirteen years have passed since (1st January 1995) India together with other 131 countries of the world had become a founder participant of the World Trade Organization (WTO). It is, therefore, a pertinent question to try to know whether this participation has borne a fruitful result to the Indian Economy. We intend to do so in terms of India's foreign trade, that is, by studying the trend of exports, imports and trade balance of visible items only. To do that we want to make a comparative study of the trend of these variables immediately before and after participation in WTO. For this we have considered two periods, namely Period 1 which is also called the pre–WTO period covering a period of seven years between 1989-90 and 1995-96 and Period 2 which is, obviously, called the post–WTO period spanning between 1996-97 and 2002-03.

A minute study of trend of our foreign trade reveals that in both the periods there was negative trade balance. However, this negative balance was more pronounced in

Period 2 than in Period 1. Again, in Period 1 between 1989-90 and 1995-96 there was 85.1 percent increase in exports and 73.1 percent increase in imports. That means, in this period, the percentage change in exports was better than that of imports. But in Period 2, between 1996-97 and 2002-03 there was 55.8 percent increase in exports while there was 56.8 percent increase in imports indicating that increase in imports was greater than that of exports.

All these information amply justify that during the period of WTO our trade in visible items did not, at all, go in favour of India, rather it had, badly, hit our economy.

It is a fact that in the post-WTO period Indian performance in foreign trade has not gone in favour of our economy. This is particularly true in the sphere of balance of trade. However, our export has undergone a major directional shift between 1998-99 and 2003-04. China's share in our total exports has, significantly, risen whereas that of the USA has come down to a great extent. These facts may reveal that the Asian Countries will be much benefited if an Asian Union in the light of the European Union is formed sooner or later.]

Introduction

More than thirteen years have passed since (I st January 1995) India together with other 131 countries of the world had become a founder participant of the World Trade Organization (WTO). It is, therefore, a pertinent question to try to know whether this participation has borne a fruitful result to the Indian Economy. We intend to do so in terms of India's foreign trade, that is, by studying the trend of exports, imports and trade balance of visible items only. To do that we want to make a comparative study of the trend of these variables immediately before and after participation in WTO. For this we have considered two periods, namely Period I which is also called the pre-WTO period covering a period of seven years between 1989-90 and 1995-96 and Period 2 which is, obviously, called the post-WTO period spanning between 1996-97 and 2002-03.

Trend of Indian Exports, Imports and Trade Balance Before and After Participation in WTO

We now intend to know the trend of Indian Exports and Imports in each of the two periods referred to above. This trend will be realized if we minutely explain the information presented in Tables 10.1(a) and 10.1(b).

Table 10.1 (a)
India's Foreign Trade in Period 1
(Unit: US Billion Dollars)

Years	*Exports*	*Imports*	*Balance of Trade*
1989-90	18.1	21.2	- 4.6
1990-91	17.9	24.1	- 6.0
1991-92	18.5	19.4	- 1.5
1992-93	22.2	21.9	-3.4
1993-94	26.3	23.3	- 1.1
1994-95	31.8	28.7	-2.4
1995-96	33.5	36.7	- 4.9

Source: Statistical Outline of India, 2003-04, 2002-03, 2001-02 and Previous Issues, Tata Services Limited, Department of Economics and Statistics.

Table 10.1 (b)
India's Foreign Trade in Period 2
(Unit: US Billion Dollars)

Yea rs	*Exports*	*Imports*	*Balance of Trade*
1996-97	33.5	39.1	- 5.6
1997-98	35.0	41.5	- 6.5
1998-99	33.2	42.4	- 9.2
1999-2000	36.8	49.7	- 12.9
2000-0 I	44.6	50.5	- 6.0
2001-02	43.8	51.4	- 7.6
2002-03	52.2	61.3	- 9.1

Source: Statistical Outline of India, 2003-04, 2002-03, 2001-02 and Previous Issues, Tata Services Limited, Department of Economics and Statistics and Economic Survey, Govt. of India, 2004-05.

The trend of Indian foreign trade can also be guessed by going through the compound bar diagrams shown below.

A close observation at Tables 10.1(a) and 10.1(b) reveals that in both the periods there was negative trade balance. However, this negative balance was more pronounced in Period 2 than in Period I. Again, in Period I between 1989-90 and 1995-96 there was 85. I percent increase in exports and 73.1 percent increase in imports. That means, in this period, the percentage change in exports was better than that of imports. But in Period 2, between 1996-97 and 2002-03 there was 55.8 percent increase in exports while there

India's Foreign Trade in Period I

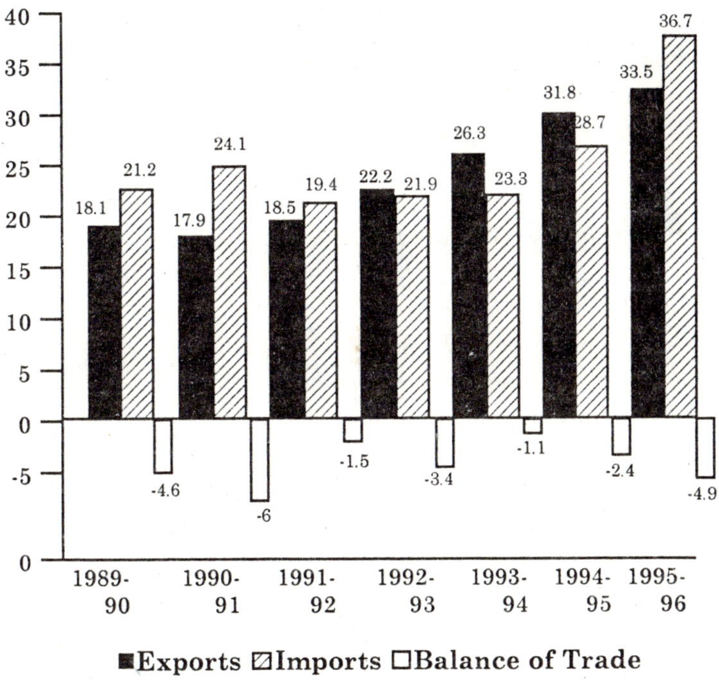

India's Foreign Trade in Period 2

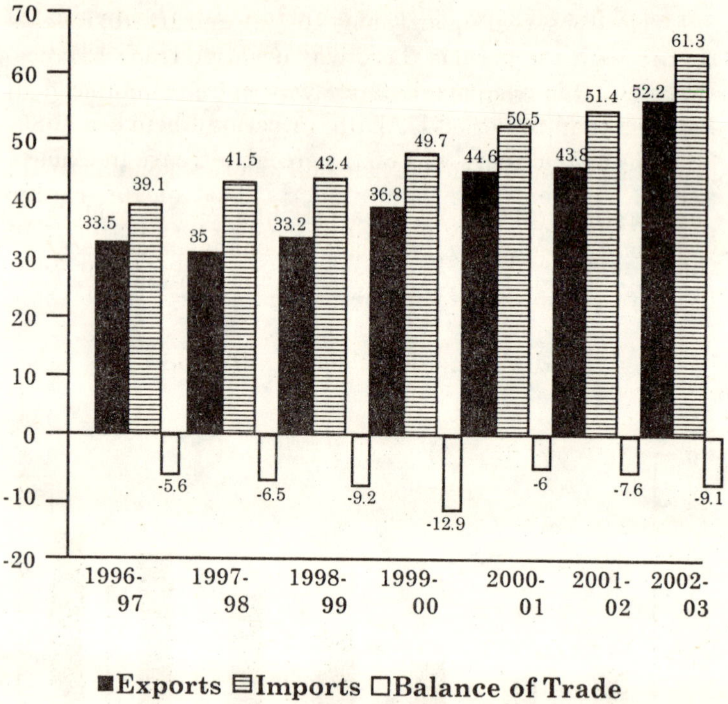

was 56.8 percent increase in imports indicating that increase in imports was greater than that of exports. Again, in Period I, that is, between 1989-90 and 1995-96 there was, in absolute terms, 6.52 percent change in trade balance whereas in Period 2, that is, between 1996-97 and 2002-03 there was, in absolute terms, 62.5 percent change in trade balance. This means that the three time series as portrayed in Tables 10.1 (a) and 10.1(b) reveal that in the pre- WTO period there was a relatively higher change in Indian exports than in our imports while in the post-WTO period there was a significantly higher change in our imports than that in exports, causing much deterioration in our balance of trade.

Besides, the annual trend growth rate of India's exports in the pre- WTO period has been found to be 13.82 percent and that in our imports has been 8.09 percent. However, in the post-WTO period the compound annual growth (CAG) rate of our exports had become 7.69 percent and that in our imports had become 5.59 percent. This shows that in the exports front the fall in CAG, in absolute sense, has been 44.36 percent in the post-WTO period whereas in the import sector, in visible items, there has been a fall in CAG to the magnitude of 30.90 percent.

All these information amply justify that during the period of WTO our trade in visible items did not, at all, go in favour of India, rather it had, badly, hit our economy.

Performance of Indian Agriculture in the External Front

Indian economy is still now based on agriculture and so it will be wise to analyze the performance of this sector in the regime of the WTO. The performance of any sector of an economy can be judged by the contribution made by that sector in the external front. So far as Indian Economy is considered the agricultural and allied products have a crucial role to play in our total exports. This can be established by the fact that in 1995-96, 19.1 percent of our total exports was shared by this sector and in the just following year this sector, sharing more than one fifth (20.5 percent) of our total exports, got renewed strength. In the next two years its share was 18.80 and 18.17 percent respectively, a more or less reasonable figure. However, a gloomy scene started developing in the last year of the twentieth century (1999-2000) when its share came down to 15.27 percent. In 2000-01, 2001-02, 2002-03 and 2003-04 its share gradually fell to 13.55, 13.46,12.73, and 11.67 percent respectively. This means that during the nine-year period between 1995-96 (when India became a member of WTO) and 2003-04 (for which the latest data are available) the percentage share of agriculture and allied products in total exports made from India, has been continuously declining from 19.1 percent in 1995-96 to 11.67 percent in 2003-04. This information can be demonstrated in Table 10.2.

Table 10.2
Percentage Share of Agricultural and Allied Products in Total Exports of India and also Annual CGR

Years *Products*	*1998 - 99*	*1999 - 00*	*2000 - 01*	*2001 - 02*	*2002 - 03*	*2003 - 04*	*CAG in 2004 over (1998-99)*
Agriculture and Allied Products	18.17	15.27	13.55	13.46	12.73	11.67	4.2
Basmati Rice	1.34	1.12	1.07	0.88	0.81	0.68	- 0.5
Non-Basmati Rice	3.15	0.85	0.39	0.64	1.48	0.73	- 14.9
Fresh Vegetables	0.20	0.21	0.23	0.28	0.25	0.32	25.8
Cotton	8.34	8.42	7.85	7.01	6.36	5.24	3.8
Jute Textiles	0.42	0.34	0.34	0.29	0.36	0.37	11. 0
Textiles	13.55	13.77	12.97	11.86	11.24	10.17	7.5
RMG	13.14	12.98	12.63	11.42	10.79	9.59	6.9

Source: The Economic Times, Kolkata, Monday 23rd August, 2004.

A minute observation at Table 10.2 clearly displays the declining trend of percentage share of agricultural and allied products in total exports of India. We notice that the percentage share of each product dealt with here in total products of our country has, dramatically, declined. For example, in case of *Basmati* variety of rice, which is very liked by the foreigners, the share in 2003-04 became almost half of what it was in 1998-99. For *non-Basmati* variety of rice the share in 2003-04 became about 25 percent of what it was in 1998-99. Similar trend has been found for other products except for fresh vegetables whose share in 2003-04 became more than 1.5 times the share attained in 1998-99.

All the previously-supplied information are the ample testimony to the fact that Indian Exports, in general, and those of agricultural and allied products, in particular, have formed a serious set-back in the regime of the WTO.

However, the recent country-wise study (The Economic Times, Kolkata, Monday, August 23, 2004) of Indian exports shows that our exports have undergone a major directional shift between 1998-99 and 2003-04. For example, our neighboring country China's share in our total exports has risen from a meager 1.3 percent in 1998-99 to 4.7 percent in 2003-04 whereas that of the USA has come down from 21.7 percent to 18 percent during the same period. With this dramatic rise of China's share in our exports she has become our fifth biggest export partner in 2003-04 against the 16th in 1998-99. However, China is not a solitary exception. Exports to Asian neighbors, in general, have significantly increased in recent years. For example, the UAE has become our second largest export partner next only to the USA in 2003-04. Its position was seventh at the beginning of the last decade. These facts may hint that the Asian countries will be much benefited if an Asian Union in the light of the European Union is formed sooner or later.

Reasons Behind Deterioration of BOT

It is a fact that in the post- WTO period our Balance of Trade has been more deteriorated. There may be a good number of reasons behind this some of which are as follows:

1. *Nature of Elasticity of Demand for Indian Products in Abroad*

It is known to the students of Economics that elasticity of demand plays a very significant role in enhancing total revenue of a firm. A firm can increase the price of its products and still get more revenue provided the demand for its product is inelastic. But in the International Market the demand for most of our products is not inelastic but elastic. Hence the moment we increase the price of the product there becomes a quick fall in the demand for our product. Thus with a reduced price we can sell more. In that case total revenue may not be up to the level of expectation.

2. *Poor Quality of the Product*

In the International Market there is keen competition and to survive in that competition our products should be qualitatively improved and those should be up to the expectation of the customers. In this front also we have not fared good. Moreover, we fail to supply the commodity up to the standard of the foreigners. We may cite the example of Singapore here. Singapore is a non-agricultural country and is based, primarily, upon tourism. But in Singapore almost all agricultural products are sold and there is a brisk sale of these products. In West Bengal lots of potatoes get rotten due to lack of internal demand. But we fail to export these potatoes to Singapore simply because of the fact that we cannot supply potatoes to the likings (say size) of the people living there. The result is that we are to be satisfied mainly with internal demand whose insufficiency seriously hampers the producers, resulting even to suicide.

3. *Bad Impact of Liberalization and Globalization*

Because of liberalization and globalization lots of foreign products have flooded our economy and this has spread a very bad impact upon us. Our contact with Western countries has, gradually, been increasing and large number of people, particularly those living in urban areas, have acquired consumption habits of the foreign countries. The desire to purchase articles of conspicuous consumption has spread like a contagious disease from which even the rural areas have not been spared. People have accustomed to consume more and more foreign products even at the cost of saving and this has led to a fall in household saving.

4. *Continuous Pressure from Developed Countries*

In most cases the developed countries want to keep the developing ones including India under constant pressure. To achieve success in their attempt these countries impose severe constraint, which, the developing countries feel, are not possible to abide by. The developing countries raise hue and cry against decisions unfavourable to them in various Ministerial Meetings of the WTO. But no positive negotiation does, ultimately, take place. To safeguard the interest of the developing countries the developed countries should be more liberal and should come forward to the rescue of the developing countries like India.

Conclusion and Suggestion

On the first day of January 1995 just after the most comprehensive but the most contentious GATT (General Agreement on Tariffs and Trade) Trade round was concluded, the first and the most powerful trade regulatory agency, namely WTO came into existence. Before the setting up of the WTO international trade in merchandise was guided by the rules and provisions of the GATT which envisaged that poor Third World Nations having comparative advantage of producing agricultural goods will freely trade these goods with rich countries' industrial goods. At the beginning the GATT recognized that under no circumstances would the interests of the Third World Nations be sacrificed in any adjustment process adapted from the growth of the global economy. However, this idea was almost abandoned. The WTO marks the establishment of a legal and institutional base for international trade that had been earlier absent under GATT. WTO provides a platform from which trading nations among countries can evolve through collective debate, negotiation and adjudication. In practice, however, this is not being followed. As a result, the developing countries have been facing tremendous difficulties in international markets. India is not an exception to this difficulty.

India's exports have been consistently rising during the 1990's. No upward break in the export trend has been visible in the Post-Uruguay round era. Our exports, in general, and exports of agricultural and allied products, in particular, have been severely jeopardized in the post-WTO regime. The last five Ministerial Conferences of the WTO have not produced good results in favour of the developing countries. However, such conferences have proved that many problems of the weaker nations can be addressed through their united effort and active participation in the democratic functioning of the WTO. Therefore, what is necessary now is strengthening the international forum through effective beginning on the basis of technology of the developing countries.

It is a fact that in the post-WTO period Indian performance in foreign trade has not gone in favour of our economy. This is particularly true in the sphere of balance of trade. However, our export has undergone a major directional shift between 1998-99 and 2003-04. China's share in our total exports has, significantly, risen whereas that of the USA has come down to a great extent. These facts may reveal that the Asian Countries will be much benefited if an Asian Union in the light of the European Union is formed sooner or later.

REFERENCES

1. Bhukta, Anindya (2004): "Agricultural Growth and Food Security: A Post-Reform Picture", *Economic Affairs,* Vol, 49, Qr. 3, September.
2. *Census of India,* 2001.
3. Chadha, G.K. (2000): "Indian Economy under the WTO Regime: Happenings, Non-happenings and Missing Links", *The 83rd Conference Volume of the Indian Economic Association.*
4. Datt, R. and Sundharam (2003): *Indian Economy,* S. Chand and Company, New Delhi.
5. Dutta, B. C. (2004): "Free Trade Policy", *The Statesman,* Kolkata, November 10.
6. *Economic Survey,* Govt. of India 2001-02, 2002-03 and 2003-04.
7. Konar, D. N. (2004): *The Scenario of Population Growth in India,* Akansha Publishing House, New Delhi.
8. Konar D. N. (1997): "Trend of Indian Agriculture in the Post-Independence Period", *Artha Beekshan,* Vol. 6, No.2, December.
9. Konar, D. N. (2004): "Performance of Indian Agriculture in the first decade of WTO" paper presented at the IIDS 6th International Seminar held at Colombo, Sri Lanka during November 27-28,2004.
10. Mukhopadhyay, M.S. Somasri (2000): "The Uruguay Round and India's Export Response", *The 83rd Conference Volume of the Indian Economic Association.*
11. Radhakrishna, R. (2002): "Agricultural Growth, Employment and Poverty: A Policy Perspective", *Economic and Political Weekly,* Vol. 37, No.3.
12. *Statistical Outline of India,* 2002-03, 2003-04, Tata Services Limited, Department of Economics and Statistics.
13. *The Economic Times,* Kolkata, 23rd August, 2004.

11

Regional Cooperation for a Better India

[Abstract

Economic co-operation among a number of countries having some common characteristics has become one of the dominant features in the Post–Second World War Period (1939-1945). Like other parts of the globe there has been a movement for regional co-operation in Asia. The Association of South East Asian Nations (ASEAN) estabiished in August 1987 by five South East Asian Countries, namely Thailand, Philippines, Indonesia, Malaysia and Singapore is an Organization meant for the promotion of regional co-operation in the economic, social, cultural and technical fields. Another example of regional co-operation in Asia is the establishment of South Asian Association for Regional Co-operation (SAARC) at a regional summit meeting in Dhaka in December 1985.So more than twenty two years have passed since the SAARC was established. Hence it is imperative on our part to exarnine whether this regional co-operation has been helpful for the furtherance of

*Indian Economy. It appears, prima facie, that this co-operation has helped our economy. This can be established by the fact that between **1998-99** and **2002-03** the annual trend growth rate of Indian exports across the world had been **11.4** percent while during the same period that trend growth rate across the SAARC countries had been **15.92** percent. However, to substantiate this phenomenon a deep probe into the study is needed.*]

Introduction

The purpose of this chapter is to study whether regional co-operation attained in the Dacca Summit in December 1985 in the form of the formation of SAARC has benefited the Indian Economy. The paper has been divided into a number of sections. Section one deals with the introduction dwelling on the historical perspective of the formation of the SAARC. Section two discusses the time series analysis of India's foreign trade across the world. Section three analyses India's trade across the SAARC countries. Section four discusses the features of India's foreign trade within the SAARC countries. Section five deals with attempts to enhance inter-SAARC Trade. Section six dwells on constraints to trade expansion. Finally, section seven mentions a few prescriptions to strengthen the intra-SAARC trade.

Section 1: Historical Perspectives of the Formation of the SAARC

Economic co-operation among a number of countries having some common characteristics has become one of the dominant features in the post-Second World War period (1939-45). Numerous regional Economies' alliances have taken shape after the Great War. Of these mention may be made of the Organization of European Economic Cooperation (OEEC) founded in 1948, the European Economic Community (EEC) or the Common Market starting in 1959 (of late, this is known as the European Union), the European Free Trade Association (EFTA). These are the typical examples of regional co-operation developed in Europe. Among less developed countries also a movement for greater economic co-operation has been noticed. The Latin American Free Trade Association (LAFTA) set up in 1961 is one of the oldest and the largest such Associations. The Central American Common Market (CACM) started in 1966, the Caribbean Economic Community (CARECOM) established in 1973, the Economic Community of West African States (ECOWAS) established in 1975, the East African Community (EAC) and the Arab Common Market are the glaring examples of regional economic co-operations among the less developed countries. In this respect the continent of Asia, the largest continent in the world, is not lagging far behind and there has been a movement for regional co-operation in Asia also. The Association of South East Asian Nations (ASEAN) established in August 1987 by five South East Asian Countries, namely Thailand, Philippines, Indonesia, Malaysia and Singapore is an organization meant for the promotion of regional co-operation in the economic, social, cultural and technical fields. The Gulf Co-operation Council (GCC) established in 1980 is an example of regional co-operation move in Asia. A relatively recent example of regional co-operation in Asia is the establishment of South Asian Association for Regional Co-operation (SAARC) at a regional summit meeting held in Dacca in the month of December, 1985. The establishment of SAARC has been an important landmark in the history of inter-regional relations. Seven countries of South Asia, namely Bangladesh, Bhutan, India, Maldives, Nepal, Pakistan and Sri Lanka are the members of this regional cooperation. In the charter of SAARC adopted at the Dacca Summit it is stated that SAARC is "desirous of promoting peace, stability, amity and progress in the region through strict adherence to the principle of non-use of force and peaceful settlement of disputes". It also calls for "fostering mutual understanding, good neighboring relations and meaningful co-operation in the region." The following are the basic objectives for the formation of the SAARC:

(a) To promote the welfare of the people of the South-Asia and to improve their quality of life,

(b) To enhance the growth rate of the economy of the countries,

(c) To promote active collaboration and mutual assistance in the economic, social, cultural, technical and scientific fields,

(d) To strengthen cooperation among themselves in the international forums and with other developing countries,

(e) To promote and strengthen collective self-reliance among the countries of South-Asia,

(f) To strengthen cooperation with other developing countries,

(g) To contribute to mutual trust, understanding and appreciation of one and their problems, and

(h) To cooperate with international and regional organizations.

Section 2: India's Foreign Trade Across the World

Let us now dwell on the India's foreign trade across the world a brief picture of which will be clear from Table 11.1.

Table 11.1 displays the magnitude of India's exports to various countries of the world and also our imports from different countries of the world. An observation at Table 11.1 reveals that in the ten-year period between 1993-94 and 2002-03 our imports from various countries of the world have been increasing at a rapid pace while our exports to different countries of the world have been steadily increasing, sometimes there is a fall in it also (between 1997-98 and 1998-99 and also between 2000-01 and 2001-02). This implies that our imports have always exceeded our exports, resulting in a negative trade balance in each and every year between 1993-94 and 2002-03.

Table 11.1
India's Foreign Trade in US dollars (Unit: billion dollars)

Years	*Exports*	*Imports*	*Trade Balance*
1993-94	23.3	22.2	-1.1
1994-95	28.7	26.3	-2.4
1995-96	36.7	31.8	-4.9
1996-97	39.1	33.5	-5.6
1997-98	41.5	35.0	-6.5
1998-99	42.4	33.2	-9.2
1999-2000	49.7	36.8	-12.9
2000-01	50.5	44.6	-6.0
2001-02	51.4	43.8	-7.6
2002-03	61.3	52.2	-9.1

Source: Statistical Outline of India, 2003-04, Tata Services Limited.

During this period our exports to the whole world increased at the rate of 8.32 percent compounded annually and our imports from the whole world increased at the rate of 9.60 percent compounded annually. These two growth rates also enlighten us that the annual trend growth rate of our exports all over the world was less than that of the growth rate of imports. Obviously, this is not a good sign at all.

Section 3: Magnitude of India's Foreign Trade Across the SAARC Countries

Let us now dwell on the magnitude of our foreign trade taking place around the countries forming the SAARC. This has been brought in Table 11.2.

Table 11.2
India's Trade with SAARC countries: (Unit: US million dollars)

Years	*Exports*	*Imports*	*Trade Balance*
1993-94	897.25	113.57	+783.68
1994-95	1215.37	176.80	+1038.57
1995-96	1722.68	256.80	+1465.88
1996-97	1703.08	241. 78	+1461.30
1997-98	1612.91	234.58	+1378.33
1998-99	1678.79	465.45	+ 1213.34
1999-2000	1414.28	325.60	+1088.68
2000-01	1858.00	435.00	+1423.00
2001-02	2033.00	573.00	+1460.00
2002-03	2596.00	498.00	+2098.00

Source: CMIE, July 2000 and Statistical Outline of India, 2003-04, Tata Services Limited.

From Table 11.2 we see that India's exports to SAARC countries have been increasing. Here we notice that in 1993-94 our exports to SAARC was to the tune of 897.25 million US dollars and the same reached to 1722.68 million US dollars in 1995-96. It marginally reduced in the following year and marginally decreased in 1997-98 and slightly increased in 1998-99. Further, it came down to 1414.28 million US dollars in 1999-2000. However, from the following year there was an accelerated increase in our exports to the SAARC countries and the magnitude of our exports to these countries was 1858 million US dollars. In 2001-02 that figure improved to 2033 million US dollars and in 2002-03 it improved further to 2596 million US dollars. Between 1993-94 and 2002-03 the annual trend growth rate of our exports to the SAARC countries became 8.21 percent.

India's imports from the SAARC countries have also been witnessing the same pattern. The value of imports was 113.57 million US dollars in 1993-94 and it went up to 256.80 million US dollars in 1995-96. In the following two years there was a marginal reduction in the imports. The imports increased to 465.45 million US dollars in 1998-99 and, again, reduced to 325.60 million US dollars in 1999-2000. In the following year a significant increase in our imports from SAARC was taken note of. In 2001-02 the magnitude of our imports from the SAARC countries was to the tune of 573 million US dollars. In the following year this figure came down to 498 million US dollars.

Our trade balance with the SAARC countries has always been highly favourable, though there are fluctuations in its magnitude. The trade balance was 783.68 million US dollars in 1993-94 and it went up to 1465.88 million US dollars in 1995-96. In 2002-03 the trade balance reached a figure of 2098 million US dollars. Between 1993-94 and 2002-03 our imports from the SAARC countries increased at the rate of 16.89 percent compounded annually.

India's major items of exports to the SAARC countries consist of transport equipment, non-Basmati rice, drugs, pharma & fine chemicals, machinery & instruments, pulses, manufactures of metals, glass etc. paper and wood products, spices etc. Our major items of imports are raw jute, inorganic chemicals, fruits and nuts, essential oil & cosmetic preparation, sugar, petroleum crude & products, metal ferrous ores & metal scrap, iron & steel, spices etc.

Table. 11.3
Percentage of India's Exports and Imports Across the SAARC Countries.

Years	*Percentage of Exports*	*Percentage of Imports*
1993-94	4.04	0.49
1994-95	4.62	0.62
1995-96	5.42	0.70
1996-97	5.08	0.62
1997-98	4.61	0.57
1998-99	5.06	1.10
1999-2000	3.84	0.66
2000-2001	4.17	0.86
2001-2002	4.64	1.11
2002-2003	4.97	0.82

Source: Calculated from information contained in Tables 11.1 & 11.2.

Table 11.3 has presented the percentage of India's exports and imports among the members of the SAARC .From this Table we get the idea that barring a few years our exports among the SAARC nations consist of approximately 4.5 percentages of our global exports whereas imports among the SAARC countries consist of about 0.8 percentages of our global imports. It may be mentioned that our exports as percentage of world exports contain only about 0.70.

Section 4: Some of the Features of India's Foreign Trade with the SAARC Countries

We may now discuss some of the salient features of our foreign trade with the SAARC Countries. These are as follows:

1. Between 1993-94 and 2002-03 there was favorable trade balance in each and every year. The highest trade balance of 5193 million US dollars was attained in

1996-97, a relatively smaller trade balance of 4897 and 4894 million US dollars were attained respectively in 1995-96 and 1997-98. However, there are ups and downs in the attainment of this trade balance, though it was always favorable.

Coming to the scenario of India's foreign trade across the world during the same period we notice that there was an unfavorable trade balance in each and every year.

2. Again, between 1998-99 and 2002-03 the annual trend growth rate of India's exports across the world had been 11.4 per cent while during the same period that trend growth rate across the SAARC countries had been 15.92 per cent.

3. Moreover, between 1993-94 and 2002-03 we had exported, on the average, about 4.6 per cent of our exports across the SAARC countries while in the same period we had imported, on the average, less than one per cent (about 0.8 per cent) of our imports from the SAARC countries.

All this information is worthy of proving that India has been benefited much by taking recourse to trade within the SAARC countries.

However, our volume of trade with the SAARC countries is relatively very low. This is due to the inherent nature of these countries. These countries have high pressure of population, have low per capita income, low saving and investment ratio. They depend very much upon agriculture and also upon exports of primary commodities. There is widespread prevalence of poverty and these countries depend very much upon foreign resources for development. India is a very big country with about 1080 million of people, while Maldives is the smallest country. The bulk of our exports goes to

Bangladesh and after Bangladesh the bulk of the same goes to Sri Lanka. The volume of exports from India to both Nepal and Pakistan are, more or less, same. We import maximum from Nepal. This being the current state of affair within the SAARC countries, we can not export more to these countries. Besides, there are many political reasons which put some obstacles to more exports in the countries belonging to the SAARC. Again, indulging in more trade within the SAARC may seriously jeopardize the competitive flavor of our products. We must search for more markets outside the jurisdiction of the SAARC areas.

Section 5: Attempts to Enhance Inter-SAARC Trade

A few years after the establishment of SAARC various attempts had been taken to increase inter-SAARC and intra-SAARC trade and commerce. In view of attaining this objective in January 1996 the first SAARC trade fair was held in New Delhi to promote intra-SAARC commerce. At the same time the SAARC ministers of commerce convened for their first meeting to discuss regional economic co-operation. A group on customs co-operation was established in 1996 to harmonize trading rules and regulations within the grouping to simplify trade procedures and to upgrade facilities. In 1999 a regional action plan to harmonize national standards, quality control and measurement came into effect. A second SAARC trade fair was held at Colombo, Sri Lanka in 1998 and the third was held in Islamabad, Pakistan in early September 2001. In August 2001, SAARC Commerce Ministers met in New Delhi to discuss a coordinated approach to the World Trade Organization negotiations that were held in November.

Section 6: Constraints to Trade Expansion

There are a number of industries and areas where substantial scope exists for individual member countries for promoting industrial development through regional co-operation. This potential has so far remained unexploited due to several factors among which the constraints to trade expansion within the region have been quite prominent. A number of studies have identified these constraints some of which are as follows:

(a) Restrictive trade policies including tariff and non-tariff barriers, (b) imbalances in trade, (c) inadequate transport network, (d) inadequate communication and banking facilities, (e) resource constraints, (f) inadequacy of trade and transit facilities, (g) lack of information, business and trade contracts and (h) lack of standardization of trade documentation procedures.

Inadequacy of physical infrastructure such as power supply, telecommunications and transport (roads, railways and ports) is the major impediments to economic growth in the SAARC region. Without improving infrastructural facilities it would be really very difficult to expand trade and investment opportunities among the member countries.

Trading relations amongst the SAARC countries are affected to a great extent by high levels of tariffs and a variety of non-tariff barriers including quantitative restrictions and discriminatory practices. One of the main reasons behind the low intra-SAARC trade and the large adverse trade deficit of member countries with India is the existing high levels of tariffs and a variety of non-tariff barriers. The rates of tariff in India, Pakistan and Bangladesh are generally higher as compared to those in Sri Lanka, Nepal, Bhutan and Maldives. Besides, among the members of the SAARC there are wide variations with regard to average tariff rates. This is established by the fact that generally high tariffs are imposed on beverages and tobacco while low tariffs are imposed on mineral fuel. Among the wide-spread non-tariff barriers in the SAARC countries are fiscal taxes, quantitative restrictions, prohibitions and canalization through State Trading Organizations.

Section 7: A Few Recommendations for Strengthening the Intra-SAARC Trade

From the previous analysis we may now recommend the followings in order to have more trade among the SAARC countries.

1. The countries of the SAARC region should have to coordinate and rationalize their concentration on export especially in respect of agricultural and allied products. The countries of the SAARC region for which exports of agricultural goods are quite significant will have to evolve integrated plans of action for taking advantage of potential of additional agricultural trade. Moreover, these countries should have to consider the feasibility of active co-operation both among themselves and with international marketing organizations to draw up guidelines relating to joint marketing and market promotion of selected products group.

2. Since almost each and every country in South Asia is in the grip of acute shortages of foreign resources, it is of utmost necessity to develop a proper financial and institutional framework which may reduce the use of foreign enchange for the settlement of accounts for trade among the regional countries. Unless the purchasing power of the SAARC countries is augmented through a joint program of bringing down their shortages of foreign exchange resources and improving the net transfer of resources for expansion of intra-regional trade, the prospects of intra-SAARC trade are likely to continue in a state of uncertainty.

REFERENCES

1. *Asian Development Outlook,* Asian Development Bank, (1999): Oxford University Press.

2. Dreze, J & Sen, A. (1995): *Indian Economic Development and Social Opportunity*, Oxford University Press.

3. *Economic Survey*, Government of India: The Relevant Issues.

4. Human Development Report (2002): UNDP,OUP.

5. *India's Foreign Trade*: IBO-03, Block5, Trade Prospects of Select Markets, Indira Gandhi National Open University, School of Management Studies.

6. Konar, D.N.(1996): " Problem of Food and Malnutrition in the SAARC Countries", *Artha Beekshan*, Vol. 5, No.2, Dec.

7. *Statistical Outline of India*, Relevant Issues, Tata Services Limited.

8. *The Europa World Year Book* (2003), Vol. 1, 44th edition, Europa Publications, Taylor & Francis Group, London and New York.

9. *The States' Year Book* (2006) (Ed) Barry Turner.

12

The Extent of Human Poverty in India and Indonesia

[Abstract

Poverty is a universal phenomenon and the concept of poverty is as old as the human civilization. It is a relative term: even the richest person of a region may think that he (she) is poorer than his (her) counterpart of another region. Hence to raise his (her) standard he (she) strives to earn more and more and this leads to more inequality in the economy. It is admitted that the famous **Pareto Law** *introduced by V.* **Pareto** *in 1897 can clearly explain the inequality of size distribution (and even human capability). But earning of income which is the basic reason behind the existence of high inequality in a society is more a matter of opportunity than a matter of human capability and cannot, therefore, be predicted by the said law.*

By poverty we generally mean economic poverty caused due to the lack of purchasing power. It is widely believed that the manifestation of poverty is multidimensional in nature. Hence the estimates of poverty should be based not only by the income measure but also by a number of factors that may be called indicators of poverty. One such indicator is human poverty that is, again, due to high economic poverty. Following are the basic symptoms of human poverty:

(a) High rate of growth of population and consequently a high density of population. .

(b) Prevalence of child labour and street labour (bond labour).

(c) Prevalence of malnourished children.

(d) High percentage of children not taking part in primary or secondary schools.

(e) Sex ratio unfavourable to women.

(f) High illiteracy rate.

(g) High infant mortality rate.

(h) Safe water inaccessible to a high percentage of people.

(i) Health services not within the reach of a high percentage of people.

(j) A high percentage of people is deprived of the advantage of sanitary system.

Judged by most of these indicators we intend to examine the extent of poverty in both these countries having won independence at about the same time, after remaining under bondage of the foreigners for quite a long period.]

Introduction

Any study between India and Indonesia may be very interesting in that there are some similarities between these two countries. Both the countries had been under foreign rule for centuries. Indonesia had remained a Dutch Colony for three centuries before it finally became a sovereign State in December 1949. India had been under British Rule for about two centuries before it became a sovereign State in August, 1947. Thus both the countries had attained independence through prolonged struggle at about the same time. Both India and Indonesia are very populous countries. India is the second most populous country whereas Indonesia is the fourth such country in the world. In fact, Indonesia is the most populous nation in the South East Asia. Among the Indonesian population there are more than 300 different ethnic groups, 250 distinct languages and most of the major world religions are found there. Among Indian people a more or less similar pattern gets noticed. In spite of such diverse features in population the basic matter of both the countries is stated by "Unity in Diversity".

Notwithstanding the above-mentioned similarities between the two countries under consideration, the nature of development attained by these countries is quite different. Here we make a humble attempt to study this diversity.

The Concept of Poverty

Poverty is a universal phenomenon and the concept of poverty is as old as the human civilization. It is a relative term: even the richest person of a region may think that he (she) is poorer than his (her) counterpart of another region. Hence to raise his (her) standard he (she) strives to earn more and more and this leads to more inequality in the economy. It is admitted that the famous Pareto Law introduced by V. Pareto in 1897 can clearly explain the inequality of size distribution (and even human capability). But earning of income which is the basic reason behind the existence of high inequality in a society is more a matter of opportunity than a matter of human capability and can not, therefore, be predicted by the said law.

By poverty we generally mean economic poverty caused by the lack of purchasing power. It is widely believed that the manifestation of poverty is multi-dimensional in nature. Hence the estimates of poverty should be based not only by the income measure but also by a number of factors that may be called indicators of poverty. One such indicator is human poverty that is, again, due to high economic poverty. The basic symptoms of human poverty are:

(a) General trend of growth rate of population is high and the consequent density of population is also high.

(b) Condition of children with respect to health and education is very precarious.

(c) Status of women with respect to six ratio, maternal mortality rate and total fertility rate is highly miserable.

(d) Adult illiteracy rate is very high.

(e) Inequality in income or consumption is prominent.

(f) Social investment with respect to safe drinking water, health services and sanitaty system is relatively poor.

(g) Human development index is very low.

A Brief History of India and Indonesia

India is one of the oldest civilizations with a Kaleidoscopic and rich cultural heritage. It measures 3214 km from North to South and 2933 km from East to West with a total land area of 3287263 sq. km. It has a land frontier of 15200 km. and a coastal line of 75165 km. Andaman and Nicobar Islands in the Bay of Bengal and Lakshadweep in the Arabian Sea are parts of India. India, accounting for only 2.42% of the global land has provided shelter to about 17% of the world population. Naturally, ours is an over-populated country. In fact, three of its metropolitan cities, namely Mumbai, Kolkata and Delhi have been placed the fifth, seventh and ninth rank respectively in the list of seventeen mega cities (having population of ten million and more) of the world in 2001. India has achieved multifarious socio-economic progress during more than sixty years of its independence.

India is a vast country where there are 28 States and 7 Union Territories. The average density of population in India per sq.km. is 324 (Census 2001) and it varies considerably from one State to another State. For illustration, it is as high as 904 in case of West Bengal and as low as only 13 in Arunachal Pradesh. It is the country principally of the Hindus as about 82 per cent of our population belong to this religion. Muslims (12.0%), Christians (2.3%), Sikhs (2.0%), Jains (0.4%) and people of some other religions also live here. The nature, progress and degree of development among different States have been vividly divergent as the States themselves are virtually different among themselves in many a respect, namely area, physical appearance, population, culture, natural endowment and so on. Consequently, some States have grown at a rapid pace and have attained higher human development index while some others have progressed at a snail's pace and have, virtually, remained backward for years together.

The largest country in the South -East Asia is Indonesia having an area of about 2027087 sq. kms. It is composed of 13667 islands, more than 7600 of which have remained unnamed and 12700 of which are uninhabited. Indonesia developed its independence from the Netherlands in 1945 though its struggle for independence continued until 1949. It was not until the official recognition by the United Nations of the Iran Barat as a part of Indonesia in 1969 that the nation took its present form. The country had followed an erratic path of development for long sixteen years between 1949 and 1965. It had, however, managed to establish its identity and integrity. After 1965 it followed a more rational development plan, maintained stabilization of the currency, strengthened the general basis of the economy and made an improvement of the so-long observed low standard of living.

Indonesia is basically a rural country with almost 80% of the population living on agricultural areas. About 50% of the population of this country inhabits the in-land wet-rice areas of Java, Madura and Bali, which have developed a highly sophisticated rural structure. Other areas of high population are found in parts of Sumatra and Sulawesi. Most of the rest of the country is sparsely settled by tribal groups who engage in shifting cultivation.

In the early 1970's Indonesia was not undergoing rapid urbanization despite the rapid growth of its several large cities. Except in Djakarta which experienced an influx of population from the country urban growth was more a reflection of the large total population than of any great movement to the cities. At that time the urban sector contained only 17.4% of the total population of this country. The three largest cities Djakarta, Surabja and Bandung all are on Java where concentration of most people is found. The other three important cities are Medan and Palembang on Sumatra and Makasar on Sulawesi. These six cities may be considered as metropolitan areas rather than large provincial towns, containing the major government, financial and business offices. Other large cities such as Padang, Jagiakarta and Semarang are centers of the provincial and regional government and local trade and have limited international ties or contact with foreign business. Djakarta, a megacity with a population of 11.4 million in 2001, has been placed the twelfth rank in the list of seventeen megacities of the world in 2001.

A Short Profile of India and Indonesia on the Basis of the Indicators of Human Poverty

A brief description of India and Indonesia on the basis of the already-mentioned indicators of human development can now be made. In doing so we should, first of all, concentrate our attention on the population of these countries and the children of such countries. This is because the size of population of a country, how it has been growing and is likely to grow in the future are some of the basic facts which largely influence every sector of economic and social development of a country. It is rightly said that the child is the father of the nation and to-day's children are tomorrow's leaders of the nation. Hence, the future of a nation depends very much upon health and proper education of the children of that nation. It is because of these reasons that we have given much emphasis upon the growth of population and the matters relating to children of the two countries concerned in dealing with poverty.

A. *Trend of Population Growth*

India with a population of 1033.4 million on 1.3.2001 has been the second most populous country while Indonesia with a population of 213.6 million on 1.7.2000 has been the fourth most populous country of the world. This means that Indonesia's population is about 20.7% of that of India. India shares 16.87% of the world population with only 2.5% of the global land while Indonesia shares 3.5% of the world population with 1.52% of the global land. The density of population, that is , the number of people living per square km. in India in 2001 was 324 while that in the case of Indonesia was 118. Between 1991 and 2001 the absolute increase in population in India was 180.7 million which is greater than the total population of Brazil, the fifth most populous country of the world. Between the same period the absolute increase in population in Indonesia was about 31.4 million. These statistics thus confirm that the pressure of population in India is far greater than that of Indonesia.

In the world population has been increasing each year by about 80 million while in India this increase is about 18 million. The total population of Australia is 18 million. Thus from the standpoint of population growth India has been adding one Australia every year. Between 1990 and 2000 the world population had grown exponentially at an annual rate of 1.4%. This rate in case of India was 1.96% and in case of Indonesia was 1.6%. This means that the annual compound growth rate of population in case of both India and Indonesia was greater than that of the world.

B. ***Condition of Children***

Let us now portray some of information relating to children in these two countries. These have been presented in Table 12.1.

Table 12.1
Children of India and Indonesia

Countries	*Percentage of low birth weight children*	*Percentage of under-weight children age 5*	*Infant mortality rate (per 1000 live births)*		*Under Five mortality rate (per 1000 live births)*	
	1990-94	*1990-98*	*1970*	*1998*	*1970*	*1998*
India	33	53	130	69	206	105
Indonesia	14	34	104	40	172	56

Source: World Development Report, Relevant Issues.

Table 12.1 authenticates the precarious condition of children born of India. It is seen from this Table that about a decade ago 33 percent of children born of Indian mothers remained underweight. Mal-nourishment of children, anaemia of mothers etc. may be reasons behind such a sorry state of affair. In this respect the position of Indonesia is really praiseworthy. In India the percentage of under-weight children under age five is also high. In this field Indonesia's performance is good. A clear symptom of poverty gets reflected through low birth weight children.

A significant symptom of wide-spread poverty lies with the higher infant mortality rate, that is, the annual number of deaths of infants under one year of age per 1000 live births. This rate was very high in both India and Indonesia in 1970. However, in the closing phase of the twentieth century both countries had significantly reduced this rate, though the achievement of Indonesia is superior to that of India. The same pattern has been found in the case of under five mortality rate.

C. *Poor Status of Women in the Society*

A very important indicator of miserable poverty is the poor status of women in the society. This is expressed through a very unfavorable sex ratio, high maternal mortality ratio, high fertility rate and a high percentage of pregnant women in the reproductive age of 15-49 with anaemia. All these relevant information are contained in Table 12.2.

Table 12.2

Sex Ratio, Maternal Mortality Ratio, Total Fertility Rate and Pregnant Women with Anaemia in India and Indonesia

Countries	*Sex Ratio*		*Maternal mortality Ratio per 100000 Live birth*	*Total Fertility Rate*		*Percentage of pregnant women aged 15-49 with anaemia*
	1951	*2001*	*1990 - 98*	*1975-80*	*1995-00*	*1985-86*
India	946	933	410	4.8	3.1	88
Indonesia	1016	1004	450	4.7	2.6	74

Source: World Development Report, Relevant Issues.

Sex composition of the human population is one of the basic demographic characteristics and this is extremely vital for any meaningful demographic analysis. Changes in sex composition largely reflect the underlying socio-economic and cultural patterns of a society in different ways. Sex ratio, that is, the number of females per one thousand of males, is an important social indicator to measure the extent of prevailing equity between males and females in a society at a given point of time. This ratio in India has been always unfavourable to women. It is surprising to note that in 1901 this ratio was 972, in 1951 this fell to 946, in 1991 this further fell to 927 and in 2001 this improved only to 933. In 1951 this ratio in Indonesia was 1016, a highly favourable ratio to women. But in 2001 there has been a fall in this ratio, it had come down to 1004–still it is an ideal ratio. So in this respect Indonesia is in an advantageous position. An unfavourable sex ratio is one of the basic symptoms of poverty of a country. It is this acute poverty that makes a certain amount of bias in the allocation of many essential items, viz. food, health services and medicines etc. Again, it is because of this poverty that girls in many parts of India are tolerated rather than welcome–they are looked upon as unwanted children.

One likely consequence of extreme poverty is the early marriage of the girls, the possible effects of which manifest themselves in the relatively large number of deaths among women in the reproductive age of 15-49, due partly to physical incapability to bear the burden of motherhood. This, along with extremely poor or non-existent medical facilities in remote areas and absence of pre-natal and post-natal care, accounts for high maternal mortality ratio as revealed in Table 12.2. This ratio is very high in Indonesia while the position of India in this respect is relatively better.

Acute poverty, high infant mortality rate and strong desire for having male children have led to an enhancement of total fertility rate (the average number of children that would be born alive to a woman during her reproductive age if she were to bear children at each stage in accordance with the prevailing age-specific fertility rates) which was almost identical in India and Indonesia during 1975-80. Both the countries had significantly reduced this rate during the period 1995-2000. However, much is desired from India. Another symptom of poverty gets reflected through pregnant women suffering from anaemia which is severe in both the countries, more so in India.

D. *Poor Investment in Social Sector*

A clear symptom of poverty is found in social investment. This may be illustrated by the fact that safe drinking water, health services and sanitation are still inaccessible to a large number of people. Table 12.3 will bring this picture into light.

Table 12.3
Progress in Social Investment

	Percentage of population without access to			
Countries	*(a) Safe drinking Water 1990-98*	*(b) Health Services 1990-96*	*(c) Sanitation 1990-96*	*Health Expenditure as a percentage of GDP 1990-96*
India	19	15	71	3.5
Indonesia	26	07	49	1.5

Source: Human Development Report, Relevant Issues.

Table 12.3 prominently demonstrates that 38 percent of total population of Indonesia are still unable to get safe drinking water while in case of India this is exactly half. In India 15 percent of total population is deprived of health services while in case of Indonesia this figure is about half of that of Indian. In India more than 70 percent of population does not get the benefit of sanitation while in case of Indonesia this figure is about 50 percent of total population. It is to be noted that in India 3.5 percent of GDP is spent on health while in case of Indonesia this percentage is as low as 1.5. Obviously, progress in social investment in both the countries is in a pitiable condition.

E. *High Adult Illiteracy Rate*

Because of poverty most of the people do not have any urge for making themselves literate. Each and every person of a poor family is busy with earning something in either cash or kind to have a square meal a day. Parents get inclined to make their sons and daughters engaged in various jobs (sometimes immoral and illegal also) and they are least interested in giving them even the primary education. Themselves being illiterate and themselves being brought up in a poor atmosphere with poverty as the constant companion, the poor parents have no other alternative but to make their children illiterate. Table 12.4 will highlight the level of adult illiteracy in the countries under our consideration.

Table 12.4
Adult Illiteracy Rate in India and Indonesia in percentage (Age 15 and above), 2000

Countries	*Rate*
India	42.8
Indonesia	13.1

Source: World Development Report,2003.

Table 12.4 demonstrates that in the matter relating to dissemination of education Indonesia has achieved a great success. In this connection India is far behind because in this continent-like country about 43 percent of adult people are illiterate. It is a fact that poverty is the root cause behind massive illiteracy in India. It is simultaneously true that because of illiteracy the people fail to get their lot improved to a good extent.

F. *Inequality in Income or Consumption and Massive Poverty*

In both the countries the inequality in income or

consumption is very acute. This is particularly true to India. A natural consequence of such inequality is the widespread poverty. This information will appear in Table it 12.5.

Table 12.5
Percentage Share of Income or Consumption and Population Below the Poverty Line

Countries	*Percentage share of income or consumption of*		*Population below poverty line in percentage 1997*
	Lowest 10% people	*Highest 10% people*	
India (1997)	3.5	33.5	35.0
Indonesia (1999)	4.0	26.7	27.1

Source : World Development Report, 2003.

It is seen from the above Table that more than one third of the Indian people live below the poverty line while in Indonesia about 27 percent of population live below the poverty line.

It is reported that most of the hungry people of the world live in India. A skew pattern of share of income or consumption in both the countries is one of the basic reasons behind this massive poverty. It is a matter of great pity that in India the poorest 10 percent of the people has only 3.5 percent of income or consumption while richest 10 percent of them enjoy 35 percent of income or consumption. In Indonesia the picture is slightly better. A highly skewed distribution of income cannot but keep innumerable people in the doorstep of poverty.

Conclusion

Judged by the above-mentioned criteria of the prevalence of human poverty and economic poverty we note that there is wide difference in the attainment of development between the two countries. It is because of this reason that India and

Indonesia have attained different human development indices: the human development index attained by India in 1998 was 0.563 while that attained by Indonesia in the same year was 0.670. The position of Indonesia at the closing phase of the twentieth century has been extremely superb in comparison to that attainted by it in 1970. Table 12.6 will illustrate such a rosy feature.

The Table shows that on the supply of nutrition to the people the position of India was , in general, superior to that of Indonesia. But within the next three decades or so the position has, effectively, gone in favour of Indonesia. It is also to be noted that in 1975 only 19.4 percent of total population of Indonesia was in urban areas and in the same year 21.3 percent of the Indian people was urbanized. But in 1998 the figure for Indonesia had been 38.3 percent, the corresponding figure for India being 27.7 percent. It has been estimated that by 2015, about 36 percent of the Indians will be urbanized while more than 52 percent of the Indonesians will be urbanized.

Behind the all-round development in Indonesia lies an effective check on the growth rate of population. This may be explained by the fact that between 1961 and 1971 population had grown in that country at an annual compound rate of 2.08%. But between 1975 and 1998 there was a fall in this rate from 2.1% to 1.8%. This is attributed to the successful implementation of the family planning programme embarked upon in the 1970's. The success story of the all-round development in Indonesia has been reflected through an enhancement in the life expectancy at birth which increased from 52.8 years attained during 1975-80 to 65.1 years attained during 1995-2000. Coming to the scenario of India we see that the annual compound growth rate of population between 1951-61, 1961-71, 1971-81, 1981-91 and 1991-2001 had respectively been 1.96,2.20,2.22, 2.14 and 1.96 percent. This means that though India is a pioneer in

Table 12.6

Supply of Nutrition in India and Indonesia

	Daily per capita supply of calorie			*Daily per capita supply of protein*			*Daily per capita supply of fat*		
Countries	*Amount*		*Percentage Change*	*Total grams*		*Percentage Change*	*Total grams*		*Percentage Change*
India	1970	1997	1970 - 97	1970	1997	1970-97	1970	1997	1970-97
	2082	2496	19.9	52.3	59	12.9	30.7	45	46.5
Indonesia	1842	2886	56.7	42.1	67	72.7	20.9	36	72.2

Source: Human Development Report, Relevant Issues.

the introduction of family planning programme in the world, she has failed to implement it successfully. Such a failure has resulted in a dismal picture of the all-round development of India because a high growth rate of population in India has eaten into the vitality of the Indian economy. India has attained some growth, no doubt, but less development.

In conclusion, we may thus say that though India and Indonesia had attained independence at about the same time, Indonesia after overcoming the initial hurdles, has emerged to be a very prosperous nation. To-day Indonesia is sometimes called a *mini tiger* or a *cub of Asia,* the other two tigers being Thailand and Malaysia. The original four Asian tigers are, however, Korea, Taiwan, Singapore and Hongkong. Indonesia through its concerted effort, strong determination and high devotion has, in reality, made the name worthy of being attributed.

It is a fact that Indonesia has improved its human development index (HDI) to 0.711 in 2004 from 0.682 in 2000, an improvement of 4.25 percent. On the other hand, India has improved its HDI to 0.611 in 2004 from 0.577 in 2000, an improvement of 5.9 percent. Besides, in HDI Indonesia improved its rank to 108 in 2004 from 110 attained in 2000. However, India in this very field got her rank deteriorated to 126 in 2004 from 124 attained in 2000, that is, India worsened its rank in HDI.

Moreover, in Gender Development Index (GDI) both Indonesia and India improved the index during the same period—Indonesia from 0.678 to 0.704 while India from 0.560 to 0.591. In this respect also India had shown better performance. In GDI, Indonesia improved its rank to 81 in 2004 from 91 in 2000 while India bettered its rank to 96 in 2004 from 105 in 2000.

REFERENCES

1. *Census of India*, Relevant Issues.
2. Coale, A.J. and Hoover, E.M.: *Population Growth and Economic Development in Low Income Countries.*
3. Datt, Rudder and Konar, D.N. (Eds) (2000): *Social Choice and Development*, Deep & Deep Publications Pvt. Ltd., New Delhi.
4. Dreze, Jean and Sen, Amartya (1995): *Indian Economic Development and Social Opportunity*, Oxford University Press.
5. *Economic Survey: Government of India* (2001, 2002 and 2003).
6. Jones, Gavin, W. and Visaria, Pravin (Eds) (1997): *Urbanization in Large Developing Countries—China, Indonesia, Brazil and India*, Clarendon Press, Oxford.
7. *Human Development Report*, UNDP, Relevant Issues.
8. Konar, D.N. (1999): "Pattern of Development of the Majority of States of India", *Economic Affairs*, Kolkata. Vol.44 Qr.4,Dec.
9. Konar, D.N. (1996): "Problem of Food and Mal- nutrition in the SAARC Countries", *Artha Beekshan*, Kolkata, Vol. 5, No.2, December.
10. Visaria P. and Visaria, L. : "India's Population Scene After 1981 Census", *Economic and Political Weekly*, Vol. XVI No. 44,45 and 46, Special Number.
11. *The World Development Report*, The World Bank, Relevant Issues.

13

Conclusion

In the previous chapters some very key contemporary issues relating to the Indian Economy have, just, been highlighted. From such discussion it is quite clear that even after more than six decades of the attainment of independence India has not yet been able to solve some basic problems for the solution of which we have been harping upon the same string since independence. We have neither been able to make our country self-sufficient in food nor have we been in a position to control the growth rate of our population. As a consequence, the extent of poverty from our country has not disappeared, though the magnitude of it has declined to a great extent. One simply wishes that a big country like ours after more than six decades of the attainment of independence through most strenuous efforts and struggle will be capable of at least feeding and clothing its own citizens. Such a wish still remains a dream.

Corruption, in many cases, has become the order of the day. This has put continuous strain in the mind of the honest and sincere citizens—they are in a fix as to choose the right path. So there is the question: how long they will remain honest and law-abiding. They will, however, be dictated by the famous saying of late Bankim Chandra Chattopadhyay, the great litterateur and Bengali novelist, "You may be unreligious but that is no reason for me not being religious."

We have not yet paid due honour and respect to the women who comprise about half of about 1100 million of people of our country. The sex ratio, especially, the child sex ratio, has been going down and down. This is not at all a healthy sign of development as it will yield instability and chaos in the whole society. We are to take due care for arresting such highly unfavorable sex ratio. Besides, proper care must be taken for controlling the growth rate of population of this country. In this respect women have, definitely, a great role to play. They are to come forward; we are to cooperate sincerely with them and we are to continuously encourage them. It is a matter of great pleasure that the Government of India and all State Governments have been giving due honor and respect to our elderly people called "Senior Citizens"(some fringe benefits in the matter of tax, rate of interest, travelling and so on are being provided to these persons). Besides, continuous migration from neighbouring States must be forthwith stopped.

It is a fact that still now agriculture is the very basis of the whole economy of the country comprising nearly 71 percent of rural people. However, the contribution of agriculture to the GDP has, continuously, been diminishing. It gets established by the fact that agriculture's contribution to GDP declined from 36.76 percent in 1983 to 20.22 percent in 2004-05. But its share of employment declined from 68.27 percent to 56.47 percent during the sanae period. In 1983 a worker in non-agricultural activities was 3.7 times as productive as a worker in agriculture. The differential in favor of non-agriculture increased to 5.12 times in 2004-05. Since agriculture is, predominantly, a rural industry and concentration of non-agricultural activities inspires urbanization, we should expect rural urban income differentials to increase. Moreover, the growth rate of production of most of the agricultural commodities has come to decline, especially after the reform period. Sufficient quantities of wheat, pulses, oil-seeds etc. are not being produced with the consequent result that supply has come shorter than demand, leading to an increase in the price level. Many such products have gone beyond the reach of the common people. The Planning Commission has, seriously, noted it and, in fact, the Eleventh Plan aims at agricultural dynamism in India. It has been declared that "One of the major challenges of the Eleventh Plan must be to reverse the deceleration in agricultural growth from 3.2 percent observed between 1980-81 and 1996-97 to a trend average of only 1.5 percent subsequently. This deceleration is, undoubtedly, the root of the problem of rural distress that has surfaced in many parts of the country. A Second Green Revolution is urgently needed to raise the growth rate of agricultural GDP to around 4 percent. This is not an easy task since actual growth of agricultural GDP including forestry and fishing was only 1 percent per annum in the first three years of the Tenth Plan. This calls for action on both the demand side and supply side".(An Approach to 11th Five Year Plan, Planning Commission, Govt. of India, June 14,2006, p-5).

In our economy the service sector has, recently, come into limelight and about 52 percent of our GDP is coming from this sector alone. But this rate is not commensurate with the percentage of work-force employed in this sector. Besides, there is wide disparity in the salary between employees engaged in this sector and those engaged in non-service sector. This will only add fuel to the growing inequality in the distribution or income among the people of the whole country. This is, once again, a very bad symptom of development, which should be shunned as early as possible.

A growing population, especially in the developing countries of the world, has put constant pressure upon our "Mother Earth" and this is one of the significant reasons behind bringing global warming, the much talked-about present problem. With the passage of time a yawning gap has been created between the rich nations and the poor nations. The poor nations, in order to maintain their livelihood, started over-exploiting Nature while the rich ones, in order to accumulate more and more resources, also started formulating such policies and formulae as will help them pile up immense wealth for their hedonistic life-style without caring for the other world where more than 2.5 billion people live in abject poverty. As a consequence the entire world has been facing Nature's wrath for the removal of which population must be controlled and brought to the minimum. At the same time our greed for getting more and more wealth must also be put to a limit.

In order to make an improvement in the overall economic condition of the whole country we have become a member of the World Trade Organization. However, statistics reveal that during the regime of the WTO also our agriculture has fared very bad. So time has become opportune to review such a situation. The formation of the SAARC in 1985 has enabled our economy to expand our trade among the SAARC countries. However, the Asian countries will be highly benefited if an Asian Union in the light of the European Union gets formed sooner or later. Another matter may be mentioned in this context with regard to the growth experience of Indonesia and India, the two countries which got independent almost at the same time. It is a fact that in comparison to India, Indonesia's attainment in various fields of an economy has been really superb and this country has come to more limelight. Hence we should learn the lessons of Indonesia's way of coming into prominence and apply those to our country also.

Finally, we had almost forgotten the name of Kautilya, the great Indian Economic Thinker in ancient times. However, this great personality has, once again, come into picture. We should, obviously, concentrate more on his "Arthashastra" and follow the necessary prescriptions recommended there.

Index

■■■